Your Fledgling Athlete

A Handbook For Sideline Parents

by

Kurt J. Mohney

Kayjun Book Services

PublishAmerica

Baltimore

Photo by Tony Alise
Illustrations by Jim Brennemen II of Artboy Design

First printing

ISBN: 1-4137-2075-7
PUBLISHED BY PUBLISHAMERICA, LLLP
www.publishamerica.com
Baltimore

Printed in the United States of America

*This book is dedicated to all the youth of America
daring enough to give athletics a try
and to my dad and mom,
who never made me feel that doing my best was not enough.*

ACKNOWLEDGEMENTS

First, I would like to thank my parents, Vickie, and Bud, for always being supportive and continually stressing, "try again." I would also like to thank my wife, Kelly, for always giving me the time to put my thoughts into writing. Also, thank you to my three sons, Trent, Trevor and Seth for providing ample writing material as well as the proper "space" (most of the time) to get this book finished. (Trevor, this is the secret operation I was trying to complete.)

Next, I would like to say thank you to my high school basketball coach, Richard Gulbin, who was the catalyst for my high school and collegiate athletic career getting off on the right foot. Tim Anderson was my high school idol who returned from West Point just in time to beat me repeatedly after practice, and to him I owe a degree of thanks.

To my junior varsity baseball coach, Robert Fleming, I say thank you for choosing me on your team as a sophomore and allowing me to play third base on a regular basis. In addition, I would like to thank Mike Charpinsky, my varsity baseball coach, who allowed me to be a batboy as an eighth and ninth grader after I failed to make the freshman team. I also thank him for having the confidence to choose me as the "replacement" second baseman during my breakthrough junior season.

I must also thank three college coaches who played a prominent role in giving me further confidence in both my athletic and academic development. Mr. Richard Baldwin is the coach who allowed me back on to the Broome Community College basketball team as a freshman, after I had originally been cut. He also allowed me to play soccer as a senior and get a late start (three weeks) at basketball after soccer season ended. I owe a degree of thanks to Mr. Ozmun Winters, my Broome Community College soccer coach, who allowed me to join the soccer team (later in the season) after I had been cut from the basketball team.

Last, but not least, I thank my basketball coach at Binghamton University, Mr. John Affleck, for giving a person the greatest vote of confidence someone could ever give another human being. When I became eligible to play basketball as a college junior, he assigned me a starting position. Thereafter, I always gave the best effort thinking I could never let him down.

Finally, thank you so much to all my friends, who took the time to read and make suggestions on my draft manuscripts. Without you the book would never had become a reality!

Table of Contents

FOREWORD

Although not a psychiatrist, psychologist, or even an educator, my life experiences have provided me with valuable material I believe will benefit the parents of children involved in youth sports. I have seen and experienced enough over the past forty years to know how parents struggle with various issues when their youngsters first begin to participate in athletics. I have learned much based on my experiences from the fourth grade through college, which included three years of soccer, basketball, and baseball at a junior college, then two years of basketball and one year of baseball at a four-year university. I was cut from a good share of teams and yet battled back to make them at a future time. I was ridiculed for being too skinny, too frail and even "too pale" at the collegiate level. I jumped off the wrong foot for lay-ups for too many years, caught the baseball in an awkward manner, and had an ugly hook shot right through college. Many techniques I had were quite unorthodox, but my "stick-to-itiveness" prevailed helping me to overcome various deficiencies. I have ridden the *pine* (see the Glossary of Terms near the end of this publication for all *italicized* words), advanced to be a starter and captain, as well as an all-star. I have been on the bottom and the top of the pecking order. As a seventh grader, I always discouraged my parents from coming to my games because I was embarrassed at how a gold basketball jersey hung off a pair of bony shoulders. As a ninth grade basketball player a four-month process saw me claw my way up to become a member of the second team "alley cats" via the third team "rag pickers." (Can you imagine a parent in today's society being told his child was a member of "The Rag Pickers"?) From ninth through twelfth grade, I also played the clarinet in the high school marching and concert band. I took a lot of ribbing (and not all of it was good-natured) from fellow athletes, but hung with it and it made me a more well-rounded individual. Sometimes it was tough to play the clarinet in a parade or halftime show when six or seven hooligans (and fellow athletes I might add) were chanting my name from the sideline or side of the road. I was doing something I wanted to do and these peers would not make me feel any different. It was not always easy, but I battled through it. I was called "Spiderman" by a senior member of the varsity basketball team when I was a junior varsity player due to my long arms and legs. This made me feel terrible, but I never shared this with my parents. At that point, I made up my mind to become as good a basketball player as the Lord would allow. As a senior in high school, I stayed after basketball practice nightly to be punished playing one on one, by an alumnus, who happened to be my idol. This athlete had toiled for two years under Bobby Knight at West Point until withdrawing from the military academy. He NEVER let me beat him and I hated him for it, but it helped me become a much better player. Two first-year high school teachers, both former college players, used me as a goalie to hone their skills for a local recreation league. I was a much better varsity *keeper* because of this, and had a bruised chest and jammed fingers to show for it. No one in our league could put a ball on the net with the speed those two could! I can remember some teammates telling me these teachers were showing off and not to give them the satisfaction. I almost walked off the field with the rest of the team because I was sure these teammates were correct at times. However, in retrospect

I am glad I hung in there and continued trying to block the barrage of shots on goal. These very unpleasant occurrences actually paid off. I guess one could say I paid my dues, but at times, it was no fun and often downright hurtful. At some point in time, a young athlete will probably have to pay his dues, but one improves by playing against better players.

I have coached various age groups and witnessed some unbelievable things transpire, mainly because of the parents. Thank goodness cooler heads have always prevailed in these instances. As parents, we should often remind ourselves to set a good example at any cost. Sometimes this can be extremely difficult, but we must strive to accomplish it. Unfortunately, with today's media, the well-behaved majority never make any headlines, but the ill-behaved now seem excessive. It is becoming evident that many parents need some education and training about how to keep youth sports in the proper perspective. Arguments are commonplace, but recent occurrences within our country over the past several years raise a cause for concern. The fights and violent brawls have no place in sports and adults should be setting an example. All parents, spectators, coaches, officials, and administrators must work to ensure that events never spiral out of control.

From the very first time your child participates in youth sports various types of decisions will be made which you do not agree with and many will be completely out of your control. At times, it may become an emotional roller coaster ride for you, as well as for your child. This publication is an attempt to help you to understand, and perhaps even address particular situations you may even be able to control. Just as importantly, it may help you cope with certain developments you have no control over. Notice I said, "to cope," as you may not always understand why a coach, fellow parent, or even an official behaves the way they do. Sometimes, as when in a volatile situation with a spouse or your child, you must walk away, count to ten, or even say a prayer before you react. Then try to focus on the fact that in the grand scheme of life the issue is probably insignificant. You must ask yourself, "This is all occurring over a child's game?"

I realize that many articles have been written and numerous web sites exist that address issues regarding youth sports. However, the scope of the articles and web sites are generally very limited and may only address a specific sport or subject. This book attempts to address most of the situations you will encounter once your youngster begins to participate. It should be a helpful guide to have at your fingertips to help you realize what to expect and how you should react. It might even be best to read it once **before** your child ever sets foot onto a *field of play*. I have written my thoughts and advice from the viewpoint of a parent and coach. I am also a former athlete who toiled long and hard only to achieve desired results very late in the high school years and throughout college. I feel that being a *late bloomer* has given me a much better perspective on the importance, or lack of importance, of athletics. This publication should help the parents of young athletes from preschool through middle school and perhaps beyond. Whatever your definition of success may be for your child as he participates at the youngest of age levels, I implore you never to take anything for granted. Early "success" or "failure" is no guarantee this is how it will be ten years down the road. The references to my high school and collegiate years help to illustrate how many situations may be repeated and the various experiences I encountered are used to drive home important points. After your child has acquired various skills, as well as years of experience and advice, he will decide what is of real interest and value to him. He will then make a choice and pursue the avenue that suits him best.

PLEASE NOTE: For purposes of simplicity (and perhaps due to the fact I have three sons) all references to athletes will be in the masculine gender. Wherever "he" or "him" is referenced, "she" or "her" may be substituted.

REFLECTION

Over 20 years ago, my dad penned something in a stenographer notebook helping stimulate me to write this book. Dying of lymphoma in a local hospital, he must have spent some of his last days writing his five children what I am sure he believed was some important advice. A portion of dad's advice to me was related to athletics.

Despite seeing hundreds of athletic contests when my behavior was never an issue, one particular recreation basketball league game at the downtown YMCA three or four years prior to his death, must have been forever etched in my dad's mind. After I had been disqualified due to what I felt was my fourth foul (instead of a fifth) I marched by the official scorer's table, towards my team bench, and banged my fist on the table startling everyone nearby. My dad wrote the following a few years later:

"Watch your temper. A basketball game is just a game and your character and integrity are worth much more than winning an argument."

Hobert J. "Bud" Mohney

Wow! My dad had seen me play almost 200 basketball games in a seven-year high school and college career yet this one episode apparently stood out for him as no other. He did not write me about a thirty-point game as a collegiate basketball player or my two home runs as a schoolboy. He did not applaud

15

me for any most valuable player or all-star awards. He penned me advice about controlling my temper. While dying, THIS is what he remembered most and wanted me to learn from it. My athletic "career" was over now and any past accolades were history and really of no value. The lack of self-restraint is what could have affected the rest of my life. I was almost thirty years old when I received this note from my mother after my dad passed away at age fifty-five. This small piece of paper is now framed and is hung in my office at home. My tantrum lasted for just a few seconds, but just like a drunk driver, careening across a double yellow line, those few seconds could have made a major difference in my life if I had not gotten control of myself. I had long since apologized to the scorer and the appropriate YMCA officials by the time I had received my father's note, but the deed had been done and I was still embarrassed about it. Presently, what I occasionally see at youth sporting events, in my surrounding community, embarrasses me in much the same way as I embarrassed my dad at the local YMCA on that winter evening. (Moreover, I am from what I consider a well-educated, middle class community.) After participating in so many contests as a high school and college athlete I am fairly *thick skinned*, but can readily see why parental behavior is such a concern for so many youth groups, officials, and administrators. I have been involved in numerous situations over the years and will explain how I have dealt with each one. These episodes occurred from grade school right up through my college years. Keep in mind my suggestions are not panaceas for each trial that develops and the proposed solution might not be applicable to every situation. However, some of the examples might allow parents or guardians to see another viewpoint or stimulate a thought, which may be helpful when reacting to a subjective decision made by a coach or game official. At times, you may have to take a few deep breaths and then repeat to yourself: "It is just a game, it is just a game, it is just a game. Don't ruin a reputation over something so insignificant." The various situations have occurred since youth sports began and with no pun intended, only the "characters" will change. Believe me when I say that you will encounter many characters and witness various performances by them. I have experienced it! You must learn early on to laugh some of it off or you may cause yourself much anxiety. You will also learn much more about your friends once they become coaches or spectators at their child's youth sporting events.

It is very important for a parent to remember that the young athlete is successful because he is a member of a cohesive unit called a team. Your fledgling athlete does not have to hit a home run, score ten points or three touchdowns to be considered successful. He may even think the best part of being a member of a team is the uniform. Do not be surprised if getting together with the team for pizza or ice cream after the game is the highlight of your child's day. Being a member of the team and having fun is what is important.

Many unpleasant occurrences might be avoided if "sideline parents" and coaches recalled a modified version of my dad's simple two sentences of advice:

"Watch your temper. A game is just a game and your character and integrity are worth much more than winning an argument."

THE BENEFITS

Some grueling family schedules are often the result of young children participating in youth sports programs. Many parents may often wonder if it is worth the hustle, driving, eating on the run, and extra time and effort these programs require. A sports program can provide everlasting benefits for our youngsters, but it should not always be at the expense of family relationships and family time. For example, it would not be a good idea for a twelve-year-old to be involved in youth basketball and baseball, youth choir and band all at once. Something has to give or in most cases, family togetherness will suffer. The word is BALANCE. Just as it is important for adults, it is at least as important for children. Sit down with your child and ask how he feels about everything. Step back from the hustle and bustle and converse with him. Does he miss something? How does he feel about school? Is he well rested? Would he be better off WITHOUT an activity or two? A few questions such as these should put you on your way towards achieving a proper balance. It is also imperative for children to have a proper balance in their lives. If too much of an emphasis is placed on athletics, the family, academic, spiritual, or another portion of the child's life could be adversely affected.

Thirty years ago, the choices of youth athletic programs were minimal. I did not even begin playing basketball until I was in sixth grade as a member of a team in the Junior Deputy League. Deputies in our local area coached various school-based teams, which played games on Friday evenings. Other than baseball, basketball was the only sport available at the pre-middle school level. Nowadays, too many choices of sports can often create anxiety and stress as many children are entered in programs at three and four years old. I have even heard that in the not too distant future horse stables will be springing up in many suburban communities, as polo will be offered as another choice to our fledgling athletes. (Just kidding parents! I made this up for laughs.)

Although harried family schedules may result, these programs can offer lasting benefits, which transcend the competitive environment. The benefits of youth sports should not be measured by wins, goals, or touchdowns scored or even all-star teams made. A child can be exposed to competition at a very young age, but winning must not be the ultimate goal of a grade school sports program or any nonprofessional sports program for that matter. At the youngest ages, the goal of winning should be considered minuscule. This can often be extremely difficult to keep in perspective when the games begin, especially for the fathers. Let's face it. Most of us play to win and good, clean competition does have some advantages. As a parent, you must teach your child how to lose, but perhaps more importantly how to be a gracious winner.

I can site numerous examples to prove that most children under the age of ten are primarily on a team to have fun. A case in point occurred during a youth basketball game during the last few seconds when a coach called timeout to design a last second play that could win the game. After the coach had explained everybody's role, he asked the players if they had any questions. A young player's hand went up in the air and he asked: "Coach, when's our next game?" Now was this kid really focused on getting *the "W"*?

A few years ago, after I had just sent my minor league

baseball team back into the field, a player ran back to me and asked to be removed from the game. I obliged and when the inning was ready to begin, I went over, knelt down beside the player, and asked if he was feeling all right. He smiled and responded cheerfully, "I'm good, Coach, but I see the concession stand is open and I was going to ask you if I could go over and get some Nerds." If I asked this boy the score of the game, I would bet that he would not have had the correct answer. I hope you are starting to see what is important to the participants at the lower age levels.

As difficult as it may be, a competitive nature must take a back seat to what I feel should be the main objectives of a youth sports program. These objectives are often not very clearly, if at all, defined by many of the organizations in charge of such programs.

What I see as the primary objectives of any youth sports program follow:

1. Participation and Fun:

The sports program must give a child an equal opportunity to participate in the sport and ENJOY doing so. If this is not happening something is awry and the goals of the program or the child's thoughts should be thoroughly reviewed. At an early age, parents need not be overly concerned about ability levels or aggressiveness. Developmentally, both physically and mentally, a lot can change in the middle and high school years ahead. The great philosopher Plato (427-347 BC) stated that at the "earliest of ages children should be absorbed with play and the games they create." Unfortunately, in today's society, children are probably not "creating" enough of their games and when some adults get too involved, the fun is removed from the "games."

Someone once remarked about his own abilities as a nine-year-old football player:

"I was not a very good athlete, but I participated."
John F. Kennedy

President Kennedy hit the nail on the head for this is what youth sports should be all about.

2. Discipline and Organization:

Getting to practice and games on time and participating in structured "skill drills" with teammates will instill a sense of discipline and organization in the young athlete. Parents must get the child to games and practices on time with the proper equipment. If a child cannot make a practice or game, or will be late, the child should make the telephone call to inform the coach. This will help to teach your child something about discipline and responsibility. Train your child to get the proper practice or game equipment ready in advance from a designated storage area. This type of organization is essential. It will eliminate much confusion before you walk out the door on practice and game days. Also, be sure to instruct or help your child return any parts of the uniform that must be laundered to the proper spot so it is ready for the next practice or game. It is up to the coach to make sure practices are structured and to make sure the athletes know who is in charge. If you witness practices that mimic a first grade recess then remove your child from the program. It will not be a beneficial one for him. If this is the case, you must express your concern to the coach or proper league administrator. If nothing changes, you should find your child a suitable alternative.

3. Self Esteem and Confidence:

A child's self-esteem and confidence should greatly improve when he realizes some practice will greatly enhance a particular skill, or that trying something new and failing a few times matters little. The effort is what truly counts. Slight improvements and work efforts should be recognized and conveyed to the young athlete by parents and coaches alike. An occasional compliment will go a long way in helping to promote a young athlete's self-esteem. The young athlete must understand he is part of a team and the team's performance is not his total responsibility. The act of winning and losing a contest is shared amongst the players and coaches. The adults must stress there are always winners and losers. The key is being able to handle both scenarios. One vital thing to remember is the younger the athlete, the less important the score!

4. New Friendships:

Belonging to a team offers an opportunity for a child to develop new friendships outside of the classroom and perhaps outside of the present family circles, or even the existing community. A good thing to keep in mind is that children are much more flexible and buoyant than adults are. When a child branches out to form new friendships beyond his present circle of friends, it will enhance his overall social and communication skills. Even the parents may form new relationships due to a child's participation in youth sports. Always remember that this type of networking can be useful for a variety of reasons outside the sport's circles.

5. Teamwork:

Although teamwork may not be noticeably present in all

practices and game situations, a coach should continually preach its benefits. As the parent of a child at the lower levels, you will witness your share of *beehive soccer* and *magnetic basketball* until the child reaches an age where they grasp the team concept, but only after much practice and repetition. Phrases such as "one can't take it through 11 players" or "many helpers make a lighter burden" will help reinforce this to the young participants. Regardless, the young athlete must learn that teamwork breeds success, both on and off the athletic field. The phrase "there is no *I* in team" is a great one to instill in the young athlete.

THE SOCCER BALL IS OUT THERE SOMEWHERE!

6. Sportsmanship:

Controlling one's emotions and being a good sport are critical components of a young athlete's maturation process. This should merely be an extension of a child's desired behavioral skills, which should already include showing respect and concern for others.

"Watch your temper. Your character and integrity are worth much more than winning an argument."

(Remember this portion of my father's advice?)

If a youth sport's program does not stress sportsmanship, something very important is being neglected. Good sportsmanship must be practiced by more than the active participants of any athletic contest. Coaches, parents, spectators, and even officials must also practice good sportsmanship. In many cases, you will find this advice to be an extremely difficult sell, as many adults do not set a very good example and take a *cutthroat* attitude to youth sporting events.

Sports are about life and many lessons can be learned which can help a child during his life journey. Your job as a parent should be to help the child through all the experiences, both good and bad. The various experiences can be used as lessons to enhance your child's social, psychological, and athletic development.

7. Academics and Fitness:

Participating on a sports team has been linked to an improvement in grades through high school. Other extracurricular activities such as drama club and band, and even volunteer groups offer children these same benefits. A diversified portfolio of activities offers benefits over a straight sports venue. College admission counselors look for a student with a good academic record, as well as a balanced portfolio of activities.

With childhood obesity on the rise in America, another great benefit a youth sports program will provide is exercise. Naturally, sports participation will help keep your child in better physical shape (and make him a little more willing to get to bed at the proper time on school night).

THE TRYOUTS

God how I hated the words "cuts" as a young ballplayer. To me it was almost like hearing the word "death." It is a good thing my dad was so supportive. "Kurt Mohney" always seemed to be missing from the posted team lists. I was short and scrawny in my early youth and often wonder what my dad thought after I was cut from little league three years in a row, finally making it for one year's eligibility as a twelve-year-old. I remember working hard to try to become the best player in the entire minor league system as an eleven-year-old. We did win the minor league title that year and I would like to think I played a vital role. I gained a lot of confidence in my hitting ability during my final year of minor league ball and was the primary pitcher for a first place team. However, I did not recognize the advantages of what seemed to be an "out-of-the-way journey" until many years later. Any athlete must learn to view "the cut" as only a temporary setback, not a sport-ending, or life-threatening event.

I was also cut as an eighth and ninth grader from the freshman baseball team, but I remember no theatrical reactions from my father. He never criticized the judgment of a coach on any occasion. Perhaps it was his way of trying to toughen me up for things I would experience later in life that would prove to be more important than youth sports. The real answer I will never know. Even when I did squeak by "the cuts," oftentimes, I only felt the field or court during the warm-up drills. The coaches played the games to win and a player had to earn game time. Reflecting upon my dad's behavior decades later, I see his approach was correct. As the father of three sons, I have experienced similar situations. It is VERY hard at times to see one's own flesh and blood try so hard only to end up being cut from a team. It is EXTREMELY difficult not to have parental bias, but it is essential. There will be many times during a child's youth where a parent must try to view situations very objectively. It has often been necessary for me to recall my dad's deathbed advice during certain situations to monitor my anger or frustration.

A child should make a team via his own ability and effort. He should not be placed on a team solely because mom or dad watches every minute of every tryout, sits on the board of the organization that sponsors the team, or teaches at the school which "junior" attends. As a parent, however, you must get used to various biases if a child tries out for a team where cuts are necessary. I remember when a fellow parent once remarked, "A parent has to be ready to pick up the pieces." Yes, on the last day of any tryout, a parent must be available for the child just in case any emotional issues arise. A parent must be available to listen and offer emotional support, if it is needed. For any coach, 70% percent of the number chosen during a team tryout session is easy. The remaining number can be tough and sometimes it may even be a flip of a coin for the last two or three members.

At twelve years old my eldest son, Trent, elected not to play any more organized baseball and ended up joining the track team in seventh, eighth, eleventh and twelfth grades. During ninth and tenth grades, he participated in a spring wrestling program. Initially, I was very disappointed when he dropped baseball. However, as I reflect back, the "silver lining" was that my son got the opportunity to experience a couple of "individual type" sports. On a return trip to Lafayette College my oldest remarked, "Dad, the easiest thing in the world is attending college solely for academics. I can maintain the average I need for my academic scholarship with ease compared to the athletes who must devote two and three hours a day for practice and spend numerous hours on travel. I've got it made compared to them and have plenty of time for studies and relaxation."

I was surprised and somewhat shocked. I would love to have any one of my sons get an athletic scholarship, but I never looked at it from my eldest son's point of view. As far as full athletic scholarships are concerned, the chances are minimal, but if an adolescent does well scholastically, there may be a much better opportunity for an academic scholarship. My oldest made a few very valid points, and as a sports-loving father, it helped to be reminded of them.

If your young athlete fails to make a team, it is a perfect opportunity to learn about handling disappointment. This is a part of growing up. An individual will not make every team, get every job, or become an officer of every organization or club he wants to join. A child must learn to handle disappointment and recognize that not everything in life is guaranteed, nor is instant gratification always assured. (It may take years of hard work to make a team or to become an everyday player.) However, the young athlete will become more well rounded and learn how to deal with disappointment and defeat early in life. Discuss these types of things openly with your youngster. If he is cut from a team, reassure him that it is not the end of the world. This occurrence should be used as a springboard towards improving various skills or even for exploring something new, depending upon the child and situation. When the going gets tough, I like to recall a note I once found in a Chinese fortune cookie:

"One must know there is a path at the end of the road."

One must remember, however, that the path may be surrounded by briers and thickets and may even have other perils beside it. It will not be paved and it may be extremely difficult to get to one's destination. The task may not be easy, but one must stay the course.

Some communities are instilling a false sense of security in our young by creating additional teams so their son can play little league baseball or their daughter can play on an advanced travel basketball team. There are lower level leagues for the less skilled, which were established to develop players for the next tier. Many children are forced to grow up much too fast due to various other reasons. In most instances, it is not necessary to force a child to play up a level at such a young age. Let the kids be kids! Additionally, in many cases, this may be doing some children a disservice by putting them at risk. If a child lacks the proper skills or if he does not understand the position, trouble may lie ahead. Various situations could develop during a game where an avoidable injury might occur. For example, let's say a young child who is not a very good fielder is put at third base for a little league contest. He may encounter a batter who is very developed physically and who *pulls the ball* every time at the plate. The child at third base would be in danger of being struck with a line drive if he was a weak fielder. Additionally, an inexperienced first, second or even third baseman may be run over by a base runner if he has not had the proper training and instruction. (i.e. – you are not supposed to block the base without the ball in your possession) I can tell you from experience that not all coaches are aware of these types of situations and some would not hesitate to put an inexperienced child at any of these positions. Children develop at different rates socially and academically and it is no different with athletics. Parents must be aware of the disadvantages this type of expansion may create. Although at a different level, this reminds me of an early expansion of major league baseball back in 1962. The New York Mets were created and had many very young players, as well as an abundance of *washed up* veterans acquired from other teams. It was a very bad mix of players with skills not suited well for competition against the rest of the league. It took this expansion team many years to catch up with the rest of the National League. In the early years, the Mets were clearly overmatched. The manager of the team, Casey Stengel, a grizzled old veteran himself, once remarked:

"They have shown me ways to lose I never knew existed. The only thing worse than a Mets game is a Mets doubleheader."

Casey had a great sense of humor that helped him make it through a 40-win, 120-loss season! Most of us compete to win, so if you and your child are ever put into a situation such as this try to recall how Casey handled it. As a parent, you may not be able to prevent something such as this from occurring and as long as your child is not put in harm's way, you may have to deal with it.

However, you must also be aware of all the other options. In today's age, plenty of choices are available for almost any situation we find ourselves in and it is no different with youth sports. If your child seems overwhelmed, overmatched or just plain disinterested, then expose him to some other sport or even another activity. Besides some of the more popular team sports like baseball, football, soccer, and basketball you also have track, swimming, golf, gymnastics, and bowling to name a few. Start by expressing your need to other parents or to school administrators and teachers regarding other options. Give your child some choices. He will gradually select the one that suits him best. Do not force him to continue participating in a sport that he does not enjoy. If he hates doing it after numerous attempts, it would be best to move onto something else. It may not even be sports related, but not everyone is suited for athletics and there are MANY other wonderful extracurricular activities for our youth. No one should be ashamed about a child spending an extra year or two in a developmental league. Do not let your parental pride get in the way here! If the sport is more important to you than it is to your child, it is time for you to "look in the mirror." Remember to keep **your child's** best interests in mind. In retrospect, playing down at the minor league baseball level prepared me well for the future.

PLAYING TIME

Unless your child excels at an early age, he may not get the playing time a parent feels he deserves on game day. At the very beginning levels of athletics, every candidate should make the team and get a significant amount of playing time. Unfortunately for some, however, the *rubber meets the road* generally between fifth and seventh grade, depending on the type of

I'M NOT SURE WHO WON THE GAME, BUT THE PIZZA COACH BOUGHT AFTER THE GAME AND THE COOKIES MRS. HUMBIE GAVE US WERE GREAT!

team or league involved. At this time, most leagues will become more competitive and the "better" athletes will get more playing time. The "better" athlete at this age may be bigger than the rest of the children or may excel in just one facet of the game. Remember this one particular facet may make the child a "star" at this point in his life, but it never guarantees future all-star status. It is merely a momentary advantage. Bear in mind the "better" athletes at earlier ages may not have the same distinction on the day high school graduation arrives. Oftentimes, being a "star" at an early age can be a disadvantage because instead of working harder to enhance various skills, a "cruise control" mentality may kick in and the child may never develop to his full athletic potential. At any rate, a parent should share this type of information with their young athlete and stress the similarity of practicing athletic skills to working on academic activities or practicing a musical instrument. Practicing for a spelling test requires repetition, just as repetitious drills are needed to perfect various athletic skills such as dribbling a basketball or serving a tennis ball. These types of things must be done repeatedly if an athlete desires to better himself. "Practice CAN make perfect, if practiced correctly." Great athletes are not born. One may be born with some natural ability, but the better athlete will not develop or even continue to sustain himself without hard work and good practice techniques.

One thing you must be aware of is that when a team is referred to as a "travel team" the competition and time commitment will become more intense. There will generally be an announced tryout date(s), the better athletes will get more playing time, and the coaches will be trying to win the game. This may or may not be the best situation for your child at this time of his life. You must take time to discuss the pros and cons to see how making or not making the team will affect your child and your family.

Some television analysts recently remarked about the poor college basketball free throw and field goal percentages. Many experts feel the statistics are low because the players do not practice their individual skills often enough, or are practicing the wrong things. There are excessive amounts of games being played. Clark Kellogg, a television analyst and former college player, said, "Kids do not work on the individual parts of their game because they are always playing games. I mean the games go on all year long. There is never any time to stop to work on individual skills, like shooting off the dribble, or moves in the post or a pick and roll. Everything is competition. Even some of the top camps have gotten that way."

Many of the athletic programs for children between the ages of five and ten have "game fever." At this age, the children do not care what the competition is and a good skills session with a minimal amount of competitiveness would benefit the young athletes much more. Thirty years ago, as a college student I ran a community sponsored boys' basketball program that consisted of a one-hour drill session, followed by a one-hour "pickup team" scrimmage period. The children benefited greatly and were not concerned about traveling out of town or around the state to look for games. Our uniforms were *shirts & skins* and we had no official scoreboard or spectators. However, a group of boys, between the ages of eight and twelve, learned the game, played the game, and had a lot of fun doing so! I know because I always had a tough time getting most players out of the gymnasium. Oftentimes, there is no great need to go outside of the community to search out better competition at such a young age. There is probably enough competition right in your own backyard!

As a young athlete enters the middle or junior high grades, a parent must remember that not all team members will play on game day. Remember no one can play all the time! After a certain age, this becomes a constant in the world of athletics and the coach makes the calls. I understood this as a young athlete, but it hurt. However, I never heard my father ridicule the coaches (at least not in my presence) or complain about my lack of playing time. What a great example he set!

Although somewhat of a cliché, parents must continually remind themselves that just as with adults, "all children are different." No two children are the same. I repeat: "All children are not created alike." One team member may run over a best friend to score a goal, while the other may stop in the middle of a breakaway to help up an opponent who has just tripped and fell. One outfielder may be studying the pitcher and batter intently, just as the coach has instructed, while the other is arranging a bouquet of dandelions. One child may listen intently to a coach's instructions in a huddle, while another may be staring skyward at the vapor trail of a jet. As parents, we must laugh about some of these occurrences. After all, isn't it better than crying? Most of us do not have a blossoming Mia Hamm or Derek Jeter. Very few athletes are fortunate enough to make it this far. Dwight D. Eisenhower once said, *"Laughter can relieve tension, soothe the pain of disappointment, and strengthen the spirit for the formidable tasks that lie ahead."* This may help to remind parents that there are many issues more important than youth sports. A strengthening of the spirit so one can deal with important life issues seems like a viable remedy. Do not waste your time worrying about your child's apparent lack of interest at such a young age. His idea of a good game and yours may be worlds apart. He might feel he had a great baseball game if he avoided being hit by a pitch, walked three times and no balls were hit in his direction while occupying left field. There were no chances for a mistake here and he had a perfect game (in his eyes)! As difficult as it may be and despite various circumstances, a parent must always strive to keep things in proper perspective.

At age forty, I finally learned the answer to a question I pondered since I began playing baseball and it took an eight-year-old to enlighten me. It happened during batting practice while I was coaching a minor league baseball team. As I was proceeding to pitch to the next hitter, I noticed he had his head down staring at home plate. He was also using his bat to trace around the outside of the plate. I shouted for his attention and he said, "Mr. Mohney, you need to come here for a minute." As I neared the batter's box, he asked excitedly, "Do you know why this is called 'home plate'?" At this moment, I cannot tell you how many thoughts raced through my mind. My mind conjured up memories of backyard wiffle ball, sandlot and little league baseball, high school and college baseball; but the answer to the question was never on my lips. I would certainly be embarrassed, since baseball had been a favorite of mine since childhood. An eight-year-old child posed me a question on baseball I could not answer. After about twenty seconds and a quick trip back down memory lane, I finally had the courage to say, "No, Danny. I do not know why it is called 'home plate.' Why is it?"

"Because it is shaped like a house. That's why."

From the mouth of a relative babe, I had learned something. Danny had other things on his young mind that day besides how far he could hit the baseball or how many times he could make contact.

As parents and coaches, we must constantly be aware that the sport itself may be just an outlet for a young child. He may not be very concerned about how he performs. He might not be worried about how much playing time he will get on game day. Perhaps an inning or two or the last three minutes of a game would suit him just fine at this stage of his life! Your child may not end up being the starting high school quarterback or pitcher, but he may become an excellent actor or bassoon player. He may just want to get a part-time job and start earning some money after school. You must remember that children are all different and there is nothing wrong with any of these choices. The most important thing is that they are using their discretionary time in a constructive manner.

While attending an organizational meeting of a varsity basketball league interested in promoting better sportsmanship, I heard a league official remark, "We have yet to have a player come out of this league and make it to the NBA or large Division I college, for that matter. In other words, the coaches and players need not take it quite so seriously." Most youth programs across our country are probably in a similar situation. Our jobs as parents and coaches should be a little less focused on going for *the* "*W*." Unfortunately, as witnessed during league play, some of the coaches and players "got it" and others did not.

All three of my sons have participated on a seventh and eighth grade (modified) basketball team at one time or another. The league rule states all boys must play at least 3 minutes per half. As a former coach of a boy's travel team with a similar rule, I can attest to the difficulty of achieving this while still trying to win the game and keep some sort of continuity and organization on the court. Most coaches do not want to make a mockery of the game, but some may have a much tougher job than others may have if a team numbers thirteen as opposed to eight or nine. The last three on the "larger" bench may be "a turnover waiting to happen," especially if the opposing coach loves to run up the score by keeping his starters in the game. As a parent, I have "been on both sides of the fence." I have witnessed one son, as an eighth grader, get the minimal amount of playing time, but have also seen our youngest, as a seventh grader, get a significant amount of playing time. However, they have very diverse personalities and their goals and expectations both on and off the athletic field are quite different. Not necessarily right or wrong, just different. One son happened to be driven by athletics, while the other son was not.

As a parent, you must step back on occasion and try to view things from an unbiased point of view. Try putting your emotions aside and yourself in the seat of the coach. If you were asked to put the best team on the floor, would your child be one of the starters? Where would he be in the team pecking order? If it is troubling you, ask your child his opinion. Usually even the youngest of athletes is very knowledgeable in regards to the ranking of his ability level. It may surprise you! He will be very honest. HE is the one who practices and competes against his peers and knows how he performs. Many leagues now require each player to play a certain amount of time, even at the sixth, seventh and eighth grade levels. In "the old days," playing time at this age was earned based on skill level and might still be a good idea, since not all coaches play by the same rules. Guaranteeing a child a specified amount of playing time at an intermediate level is not always a favorable experience. The ability level of your young athlete will probably influence how you feel regarding this issue.

If something really troubles you ask to speak to the coach in private, make a telephone call, or drop him an e-mail. I would suggest you do not harbor ill feelings for very long, but be sure to give things enough time and a good thought process before you approach the coach. Also, be sure to discuss it with your young athlete. Try to take a thorough view of the particular situation from all perspectives because not all involved will visualize things in a similar fashion. Most coaches will appreciate you addressing a situation directly as opposed to talking behind his back to other parents. Do not sit in the stands and "jump on the bandwagon" with other parents who may be constantly ridiculing and second guessing the actions of the coach. It might even be a good idea to suggest for some of the parents to speak to the coach in private. A coach should be able to speak to any parent and explain the rationale for his actions. You may not be happy with or agree with everything the coach has to say, but will probably have to accept it as long as he provided you with some reasonable explanations. Never embarrass the coach in public or more importantly during a game. Most coaches try their best to be fair and some may be in the spot because no one else was interested in the position. At times, a parent may feel pressured and take a coaching position solely to be able to field a team. A friend's wife recently remarked to her husband, "Oh great, Chuck. Another non-paying job."

I will never forget a mother and father's reaction at a basketball game a few years back when I coached a varsity team in a Catholic youth league. One day a father of one of my players approached me and questioned his son's amount of playing time. This player, Andy, was close to the end of the bench talent wise, but was a welcome addition to the team. I felt he was getting an ample amount of playing time and stressed that Andy was only a fair practice player. He was not a very good listener and had a tendency to fool around quite often. I told the father if Andy took practice a little more seriously and worked to improve certain skills he might earn more playing time. During the practices is where a player really needs to "show his stuff." This is where a player will be earning his game time by banking good practice performances. As eleventh and twelfth graders, most of the players were competitive and played to win. In other words, at this age, "the rubber had met the road" and the players competed for playing time. I was not positive my thinking was correct, so I posed the following question to my team after the next day's practice:

"At this level of play, what should one of my primary objectives be on game day? Is it to try and put the best product on the court or is it to give every team member an equal amount of playing time, regardless of the particular team member's ability, work-ethic, or practice attendance?"

All players agreed that playing time must be earned at this level of play. It was unanimous. There was no uncertainty amongst the team. I knew for sure during a game the next evening I had not made any "in-roads" with the father because I saw Andy's mother and father openly rooting against our team. That was a sad display of parental behavior, as well as a complete lack of class. A parent should never stoop to this level. One might expect this type of behavior from children, but not from adults. These parents should not have attended future games because they had lost control of their emotions and became an embarrassment to their son and our organization. I had to deal with this situation as a volunteer coach, despite not having any of my children on the team. There was no reason for me to show favoritism of one player over another and yet this small confrontation developed.

In a situation such as this, perhaps it might be a good idea for a parent(s) to ask the child what his thoughts are regarding the team. Is he having fun? Does he enjoy the other players and the coach? Does he like going to practice? Does he enjoy the camaraderie and social events that occur by being a team member? If the answers to all of these are "yes" then perhaps game "playing time" is not as important to him as it is to you. Be sure to take this step before confronting the coach, as you may save yourself some time and frustration. A situation such as this may also prove to be a very stressful one for some parents.

Many coaches at the early levels will have sons or daughters playing, so an unbiased opinion regarding playing time or a position being played may be unrealistic. However, most organizations are usually begging for coaches and assistants so take the opportunity to get involved and perhaps balance some of the bias, if it is occurring. If it is not a school related organization, it is a good idea to have different parents involved for the different seasons. The same parent should not coach three sports. All children need a break from mom or dad and other athletes should be entitled to experience a variety of coaching styles. It is also imperative to recognize that playing time at these stages will not singularly make or break your child as he progresses. If your child is not upset because of the circumstance, then do not let it bother you. A parent should not fill a young athlete's head with negative thoughts or ideas. Try to stay away from this and do not ruin the fun for your child at the youngest of ages. It is very conceivable the child loves the practice sessions and camaraderie more than the games. The structured environment of an organized game may be a little overwhelming to your child at this time. The games may create too much pressure for him, forcing him to withdraw from the situation in his own way. ALWAYS remember most coaches at these levels are volunteers, as well as moms and dads. They probably have a job, are dealing with family issues, and have a full plate just as you do. Sometimes the coach may not have a very good knowledge of the game and may be learning right along with the youngsters on the team. In a case like this, your patience will indeed be a virtue.

There is a chance your child may someday be relegated to the bench as a role player or a player way down in the pecking order. If this situation arises, be sure and explain to him how much can and MUST be learned by observing from the sideline. Sitting on the bench at the secondary grade level should be more than checking out the cheerleaders, surveying the crowd, wondering what to do after the game, or complaining about why Joe Doe is playing instead of one's self. This is a great opportunity for a player to become a true student of the game. From the bench one may evaluate the opposition's defense and offense, notice what an opposing player's strengths and weaknesses are, or just observe a teammate or two he may be substituted for to see what this player is doing right or wrong. When on the bench HE should pretend to be the coach. What would HE be doing to improve his team's performance? If a player watches intently for these types of things, he will be much more prepared when he enters the game. This type of situation will provide some valuable experience to your athlete if he decides to someday enter the coaching ranks.

"Bench observers," however, are lacking at all levels of athletics. Old *tomfoolery* is much too prevalent at the end of many team benches. When a player "matures" enough to evaluate the types of things I have mentioned he will have a distinct advantage over a teammate he may be competing against for playing time.

One last issue I would like to cover in this chapter is the topic one of my former coaches used to call *bomb squad time*. I am afraid things have changed over the past couple of decades in regards to this portion of the game, but I am unclear about the rationale behind it. Many knowledgeable coaches leave starters in games long after the contest has been decided. During the 2001 NCAA men's championship basketball game the well-respected Duke University coach, Mike Krzyzewski left his star player in a game where the outcome was no longer in doubt. In the 2003 men's semifinal between Marquette and Kansas, a thirty-point blowout, some starters for both teams remained in the game with four minutes left. Did not every player on the benches deserve better? Didn't the *walk-ons* even deserve a few minutes? I fail to see the sense in this coaching decision at any level and am perplexed as to why it occurs. The players on the end of the bench would relish ANY game they could acquire. They have earned it, minimal as it may be, and would enjoy it. I know because I was once in their spot at the end of a team bench. Any coach who has ever played the game should have a good feel of when to *throw in the towel*. It is extremely important at the lower age levels that coaches err in favor of sooner than later because players are there for the PLAYING time.

ENCOURAGEMENT

If a child loves the sport, has some talent, and is willing to devote some time to practice, then a parent must never run short of encouragement! My father always encouraged me to try out for teams, but never put any extreme pressure on me to practice or perform any better. Even after being cut from the freshman baseball squad as an eighth and ninth grader I still loved the game and never stopped practicing or studying it. Over this two-year period, I can thank two of my classmates who kept telling me I had to keep trying. "You will make it next year," they continually reminded me. They implored me not to give up. I could never go and watch these classmates play, but I never missed a home varsity game at this stage of my life. I enjoyed being around the bench with the older players and it kept me close to the game I loved. In tenth grade, I tried out for the junior varsity baseball team. I had a great tryout, partly due to the fact I was trying to show the freshman coach he had made a mistake two years in a row, and made my first school baseball team. I started every game at third base and had a good year. As a member of the varsity baseball squad the following two years I got progressively better, due to the fact that I devoted much time to practice.

When I was the coach of a minor league team, which my middle child participated on, I had an eleven-year-old whose mother informed me he did not want to play minor league ball. He had just been cut from the little league team and would be the oldest player on this minor league team. I called and informed his mom I would stop by their house after work the following day, just before our first practice. Upon arrival, I asked to see Michael and he stepped up into the doorway beside his mom.

"Come on out and have a seat," I said. He did and his mom disappeared.

"I understand you don't want to play on our minor league team because you are one of the oldest?"

He nodded affirmatively and I proceeded to tell him about my unpleasant experiences with little league and junior high school baseball during my youth. Michael listened attentively. I told him I was knocked down hard on many an occasion, but got back up and moved on the best I could. It was very difficult. I shared with him a phrase that one of my coaches spoke repeatedly to me:

"Keep the faith."

I informed Michael that when all else fails he must keep faith in himself. This is essential because there is never a guarantee anyone else will. When I asked him if he understood what I meant he nodded his head up and down as he choked back tears from a set of baby blues that were glistening in the sunlight.

I closed by telling him how much the younger players could learn from him and what a great asset he would be to the team. Then I reminded him practice would be starting in one hour, but I would be there a half an hour early for those who wanted some extra *BP*. I never asked him if I had changed his mind because I did not want to hear him say the word "no."

On my short drive back home, I thought about how I could have done a better job to convince him to change his mind. When he first stepped out onto the porch, I wanted to hug him because his eyes were beginning to gloss over with tears. This would not have been a good approach for me personally because soon both of us would have been blubbering. You see I could rarely make it through an episode of *Little House on the Prairie* without crying.

Once home I got all my equipment together. I then hurried upstairs and changed into my practice clothes. Upon my way back down the stairs I stopped on the landing and glanced out the side window only to witness Michael racing full throttle toward the practice field on his bicycle.

"I'd better get moving!" I shouted to my wife. "Michael's raring to go."

Michael proceeded to pitch our first game and did a fine job. He had a lot of fun, fit in with all his younger teammates, and finished the year on our squad. A small word of encouragement went a long way towards helping a little boy regain some confidence. This was also the highlight of the baseball season, for me, during the summer of 1995.

This experience proved to be a favorable one for Michael as he continued to play baseball, as well as football, throughout his high school years. We can only imagine what may have happened if he did not reconsider. I often wonder if Michael would have continued playing baseball without this simple word of encouragement.

In today's world, there are many more activities for our children than were available twenty or thirty years ago and to the truly dedicated athlete this may well be an advantage. If your child is focused, driven and unaffected by most of the items available in today's computer age he could gradually separate himself from most of his peers with improved athletic abilities. Many of his peers may be mesmerized by many of the electronic devices on the market and thus devote little time to practicing sports or to staying physically fit.

If your child wants to try a new sport and it will not jeopardize the family "balancing act" or finances, let him go for it! I am a firm believer that at a young age the child should participate in a variety of sports. My children have played on baseball, basketball, soccer, track, football, cross-country, hockey, and wrestling teams. I never participated in any of the last five sports mentioned and knew very little about them. Did this make it wrong? Of course not! It might have been an advantage for my sons. I was able to offer a nonprofessional's point of view and was rarely a sideline coach or *Monday morning quarterback*.

Now do not get me wrong because some of the choices my sons made were not easy for me to accept. One such event occurred when my eldest, then a ninth grader, arrived home one late October day and announced he had joined the wrestling team. I can honestly say I am glad I did not have any food in my mouth because I certainly would have choked. He had "known" basketball all his life and I had played throughout high school and four years of college. WRESTLING? For a second I thought I was dreaming. I heard of stories like this before, but it could not happen in my family. After a few seconds, I knew I was not dreaming. I could not believe it. A coach had apparently said some positive things to Trent and convinced him to go out for the team. Although initially shocked I did not try to discourage him, but only asked him to give it some serious thought before he made such a commitment. To this day, I have a few friends who still cannot believe I had a son who was a wrestler. I tell them it was his choice and I did not intend to discourage him from giving something new a try. Trent wrestled for four years and did relatively well, despite beginning the sport at what many felt was a very late stage.

My dad was always encouraging during the most difficult

periods. While in eighth grade, I was unable to shoot a free throw without stepping over the foul line. I was just not strong enough to reach the basket in a conventional shooting fashion so I had to shoot my free throws underhanded. My dad stressed that it was no big deal and said using two hands was a much better way because he was convinced (or so he said) it improved your accuracy. At that time, one of the top free throw shooters in the National Basketball Association (NBA) was Rick Barry of the San Francisco Warriors. My dad informed me that Barry shot his free throws underhanded. Additionally, the biggest and strongest man in the NBA at that time, Wilt Chamberlain, also used the underhanded method. (Dad neglected to inform me that regardless of which method Wilt used; he was a terrible free throw shooter.) How encouraging and positive my father was! This gave me help to put up with some of the ridiculing I was subjected to at practices because I used this method. Somehow I battled through it all and have always been a better than average free throw shooter. Believe me, as soon as I could "ditch" the underhanded method (in ninth grade) I did! After a while, I eventually tired of hearing my dad speak of Rick Barry's free throw prowess.

Encourage your child to read books or view videos about the sport(s) which are of interest to him. Videos and books can be useful tools for learning proper techniques at a young age. Instructional videos are fabulous for learning such things as a proper golf club or bat swing, a kick or throw follow through or the proper positioning of the head while dribbling a basketball or performing a high dive. The enhanced media coverage of today's sporting events can be beneficial for a young athlete. Nowadays, a child is able to read about or may actually be able to listen to many successful athletes tell about how they were able to achieve success at the higher levels. Despite numerous professional athletes who provide poor role models, the good far outnumber the bad. Additionally, you might want to keep a blank videotape handy with your child's name on it to record college or professional contests where slow motion might have been utilized to illustrate a point or enunciate a mistake. Sometimes much more is picked up if the action can be viewed in slow motion. Soon your child may want to compile his own instructional video. Over the past few years, I have even started recording some motivational pieces on a tape to use as my youngest son nears high school age. You may also want to consider using a camcorder to film some of your child's games. Be sure, however, to make the viewing fun and do not use it to point out numerous mistakes your child and the team may be making. Try to stress the good things that you see such as all the smiles on the participant's faces. As he gets older, it may be used for this instructional purpose, if your child is a willing participant.

Persistence/determination

If playing time is not extensive, or a child fails to make a team, the parent must stress persistence. However, one must tread lightly regarding this matter. Remember that not all children are born with the same desire to persevere over what may often be viewed as an extremely difficult course. As a seventh grader, I was extremely fortunate to encounter my future varsity basketball and baseball coaches who helped me through a difficult period. I literally grew up a stone's throw from the high school and became the batboy and water boy for the varsity baseball and basketball teams. I was commonly referred to as a *gym rat*. Both of these coaches preached the "never give up" attitude which stuck with me throughout my scholastic career.

"Achievement is largely the product of steadily raising one's level of aspiration and expectation."
Jack Nicklaus

A parent must occasionally evaluate the child by asking himself: "How much time does my son dedicate to individual skills work outside of team practices?" If the answer is "none" or "a minimal amount" then maybe this is not what is important to him at this stage of life. A parent must also be somewhat patient. Just because "junior" does not seem overly persistent or dedicated at this time, it may change. Also, remember that many mediocre or good athletes have been unwilling to take the steps necessary to improve themselves. It may require too much hard work and discipline and not everyone has this internal fortitude. This type of attitude may prevail at the grade school, high school, college, and even professional levels of sport. The sport may still be fun, but to take it to the next level may be asking too much of the individual. There are a very limited number of Tiger Woods-type athletes in the world. He was mesmerized by a sport at an extremely young age. Yes, his father exposed him to the sport and nurtured him, but it could have reached a point where it became too much effort for too little reward. This is indeed the exception where a very young child is so attracted to a sport that it becomes a passion. In a case like this, a child's passion will drive the parent.

A parent must be careful of browbeating a youngster into playing a sport or problems could develop in the years ahead. The desire and motivation must inevitably come from within oneself. Although an extreme case, a New York Mets first round draft pick in 1995 walked away from a game he had played since he was five, as a twenty-year-old. Why? He no longer enjoyed playing baseball. His father, a former collegiate athlete, had put continual pressure on him to play baseball at a very young age. He had told his parents the game of baseball did not have enough action for him and tried to quit the game as a junior in high school, but they wanted him to continue. This young man had played the game of baseball the majority of his life solely to please his parents. Now at the age of twenty, he was courageous enough to make a very important decision by himself. He was through with the game!

An all-star basketball player from California suddenly decided she would quit playing after graduation from high school. She was very high on many a college recruiter's list, but her love for the game was not what it had once been. Her choice was to concentrate on her major in college and she was comfortable with it. Apparently, for whatever reason, she had reevaluated her priorities and wanted to take a new direction in life. As hard as it may be for parents to accept this sort of decision, one has to ask; "If I truly love my child I must seek what is best for HIM."

I did not force my oldest two sons to play basketball, but exposed them to it at a young age and let them play. My oldest played through eighth grade and the middle child through seventh. However, neither ever had a true passion for the game. They were not very aggressive on the court and my main advice for them was to get after the ball. The more a player had his hands on the ball, whether it be dribbling it up the court or snagging some rebounds, the better ball player he would become. Very often, they almost appeared to be spectators on the court and occasionally treated the basketball as if it were a hot potato. They would catch the ball and pass it off in no time. If any turnover was to be committed, it was going to be by a teammate.

Now my youngest, Seth, was a different story. As a fourth grader during his very first organized basketball game, he played like a bull in a china closet going after every loose ball and rebound as if his life depended on it. He went full throttle from the moment he stepped onto the court. My wife looked at me and said, "That is exactly the aggressive type of player we loved to hate when Trent and Trevor played against someone like that." It is hard to believe the three children came from the same set of parents. A year later, as a fifth grader I had asked Seth to ease up a little bit or he would foul out of this particular game before the fourth quarter began. Well, he did not heed my advice, and at the end of the third quarter, he fouled out. As he walked by me to take a seat on the bench, I reminded him of why I had told him to be a little less aggressive. He looked at me and said, "Mmmmm, I thought you got six." I merely assumed he had been watching too much of the NBA.

How can a parent know if he is pushing his child too hard? For starters, look to see if he is truly enjoying the event. Does he LOOK like he is having fun? If you are not sure then ask him. Perhaps you could even ask the coach, other parents or even your spouse if they feel you are forcing the child to participate. As difficult as this may be, if you are truly interested in your child you must take this approach. Many other choices abound in today's world. If a two-parent family is involved it is important that both agree about a child's involvement in a sport. Very often one parent may be dominant, often to the detriment of the child. This might even be the time for a parent to step back and try to take a very objective view of a particular situation by reflecting on the following:

Look at every path closely and deliberately. Try as many times as you think necessary. Then ask yourself the question: Does this path have heart? If it does, the path is good. If it doesn't it is of no use."

Juan Matus

If your child has the determination, you must remind him that becoming a good athlete is not much different from playing the piano or learning to speak a foreign language. Without practice, improvement is virtually impossible. As a child nears the junior high years, this argument holds up extremely well. If he does not make a team, he must be persistent and try out again the following year. He has this whole season, as well as the seasons in between to work on improving his skill level. Additionally, scour the newspapers and telephone book to research teams sponsored by the local churches, YMCA, YWCA, or Boys & Girls Club. As your child matures, encourage him to remain flexible to various options that may present themselves. In other words, do not let him lock himself into a particular position, especially if a coach feels otherwise. Many an outfielder has been converted to a pitcher and a midfielder to a striker by coaches somewhere along the way. Just as in the work world, if someone offers a variety of skills and is flexible the chances of success are not as limited. As a parent, try to be sure the young athlete always keeps his options open.

In retrospect, I was fortunate to have kept my options open as an eleventh grader on the varsity baseball team. I was one of six outfield candidates and during the first couple of scrimmage games, as well as our first two league games, probably averaged three or four innings a game. I was not satisfied with the situation. I wanted to play more innings! Then, however, I received the biggest break of my high school athletic career! One game day afternoon I arrived to change into my uniform and witnessed a group of teammates standing next to my locker with some pliers and a hacksaw. Well, despite numerous warnings from our coach about NOT bringing a lock from home our starting second baseman did just that and lost his key. Therefore, the master key in the hands of our coach was of no value and his lock was not coming off. The coach arrived and asked if anyone would volunteer to start at second base. Without hesitation, my hand went up and I was chosen. That afternoon I had what could be called a "career game" both offensively and defensively, and from that point on I was never displaced from second base. This was indeed a modern day *Wally Pipp* story. Imagine that, all because someone did not follow the rules and I took a chance. I could also have failed, but apparently never gave this a thought. Taking a risk always involves the possibility of failure, but the greater the risk the greater the reward.

"Show me a guy who's afraid to look bad and I will show you a guy you can beat every time."
                                                            Lou Brock

It actually turned out better than I could have ever imagined, as I was the only representative from our team selected as a member of the league's first team all-stars and repeated the honor as a senior. If I had not been flexible or been afraid to try something new I would have never been afforded such an opportunity. This occurred only because I kept my options open.

"You will always miss 100% of the shots you never take."
                                                            Wayne Gretzky

Once I got into my new position, I wanted to make sure I retained it. Although not the most sure handed or slickest fielding second baseman I vowed to never let a ball go through me. I would put my body in front of it no matter how hard it was hit. I was even laughed at by some teammates for wearing a cup. My theory was that unless it was a double play ball, where it had to be handled very quickly for a turn at second, I would get in front of the ball and go down on one knee if necessary, for my throw to first base was a short one. The bottom line was that I wanted to be at this position to stay and a ball would have to go THROUGH me to get by! I never wanted to come out of a game.

I was fortunate enough to have been selected as a first team second base all-star two years in a row despite only playing one year of little league, and never playing school sponsored baseball until I was a sophomore. Then I FINALLY made it to the varsity only to have to prove myself all over again. There I was stacked up against five other outfield candidates until I got the break I needed. I had tried and failed on numerous occasions, but a breakthrough finally occurred. If you want to read about victory prevailing over defeat you may wish to do some research about how Abraham Lincoln persevered over much adversity in his personal, professional, and political life. His attitude was unparalleled.

Lincoln once remarked while in office, *"I do the very best I know how – the very best I can; and I mean to keep on doing it until the end."*

Lincoln had lost a great number of elections on the way to becoming president. Most people would have given up, but Lincoln did not. An athlete must also persevere until he gets the chance, but then he MUST take advantage of the opportunity! He must stay the course! It may require "hanging around" awhile to get that chance. Sometimes a coach will not evaluate talent properly, but that is because he is human and will make mistakes. Evaluating talent can be extremely tough. Many a high school and college coach has seen a player leave his team due to insignificant playing time, only to see the player blossom in the years ahead at another institution.

Every parent and athlete must be prepared for various circumstances that may occur during a young athlete's life journey. While I was at the very bottom of the so-called baseball hierarchy during middle school, I know I did not have a great deal of confidence in myself and probably dealt with a self-esteem issue or two. I was not very good and most of my close friends were on the school baseball teams. I kept my eye on the prize and it made it all worth it once I achieved all-star status as a high school junior, but then new issues arose. I ran into the local American Legion coach while on my bicycle one summer evening and he said, "What's the matter, Mohney, are you too good to play on this Legion team now?" Actually, it was to the contrary. I knew many players were coming back and two school districts were supplying eligible players. I would have been content playing on my town's local Junior League team made up of players sixteen and under. I did not feel I would play very much on the legion team and did not bother to attend the first tryout session. Well, after speaking to this coach I felt somewhat guilty, tried out for the team, made it, and played regularly. (How things had changed in a few short years! In my first two years of junior league, my main concern was not being hit by a pitch thrown by a sixteen-year-old. Now I was actually going to be playing legion ball. I had "graduated!")

I always felt hurt by the comment this coach had made, although I never let it affect my play. It was very inappropriate for a coach to say something such as this to a young person who was working hard to become a better athlete. These types of comments may often be made by adults and adolescents about individuals they do not TRULY know. Therefore, they should really keep these comments to themselves. As in this case, an athlete's actions might be misinterpreted. As a parent and young athlete, you may have to battle through various "negative untruths" and continue on whatever course you have in mind! Oftentimes, one can use these types of comments as a springboard for motivation. An individual must NEVER take these comments to heart!

When I was about fourteen years old I used to play basketball at a local park and was constantly abused by a guy four or five years older. Naturally, I never said anything. This came with the territory and he was much bigger and stronger. I was a relative "pee-on" for him in pickup basketball. I was "paying my dues." Well, the years went by. I grew and he did not. I got much better and he did not. I laugh when I think about it now because every time I got out of my car to play as a seventeen and eighteen-year-old this individual would remark, "Here comes hotshot." That hurt me too, but I knew I had made some progress. I went from a "pee-on" to a "hot shot" in four or five short years and loved the new result.

I did not see significant action on any basketball team until I was a senior in high school. I worked my tail off, but as a six foot, one hundred and forty pound forward there were many other players who were much better than I was at that stage of my life. I felt I deserved to play more as a junior, especially when the coach even suited up our manager to start a game ahead of me. This was really upsetting, but I loved the game and never gave a thought to speaking to the coach about it. In retrospect, I should have spoken to the coach in private after the "manager incident." I should have asked for the same chance to prove myself that he had given someone who was not even on the team. As a seventeen-year-old, I was cut from a local community college's basketball team and was extremely disappointed. I had thought this was the end of basketball for me, but my persistence and attitude was being put to the test again. During the 1950s through the 1970s, Broome Tech (later Broome Community College) had a powerhouse basketball team, a well-known coach named Dick Baldwin, and the team was often nationally ranked. During mid October of my freshman year, the team had tryouts and again I was a casualty. I immediately found out the soccer squad was in need of a goalie and the coach was kind enough to let me join for the duration of the season.

Even as a seventeen-year-old, I still lacked confidence and certain communication skills. I did not originally tryout for the soccer team because of a letter I had received in the mail over the summer. In this letter, the soccer coach listed all the footwork drills one should have mastered before stepping onto the field. Well, I was a goalie and could not perform many of them. Instead of communicating with the coach, I decided not to try out. This was definitely a mistake, since soccer was probably my best sport, although my least favorite. I was slowly beginning to learn that a proper mode of communication could indeed open many doors! However, just as with athletic skills, we are not all blessed with the same ability and it may take years to perfect it.

Three weeks after joining the soccer squad I found out one of the basketball team's prize players was homesick and had returned to New York City. I popped a brief letter into the basketball coach's on-campus mailbox explaining my services were still available. (Maybe I was starting to learn about communication!) Much to my surprise, the coach welcomed me onto the team. This time a written communiqué had done the trick. I could hardly believe it and although I did not play much as a freshman, I worked my tail off. I tried to punish a fellow freshman teammate in practice who I felt was no more talented than myself, yet he not only played a lot more, but also started at the off-guard position! Internally, this disturbed me. Very often, this teammate would tell me to "take it easy." I did nothing dirty, but made it tough for him to get the ball and was "in his face" during most of the inter-squad scrimmages. In later years, this teammate confessed to me saying that games were a lot easier for him due to my tenacious nature at practice. My motive, however, was merely to try to show the coach he was making a mistake. Well, my sophomore year this individual was still in the starting lineup and I was the first guard off the bench. I felt no different and kept working as hard as ever, but never got an opportunity to be a starter. About mid season, this starter got hurt and I moved into the starting lineup for about 15 games, making the most of it. Once again, opportunity came knocking. My game as a starter came against nationally ranked Monroe Community College from Rochester, New York. We upset them and I contributed 18 points. I averaged about 14 points in the games I started and about 6 points overall. I took advantage of an opportunity when a door opened and performed my best.

When this teammate was well enough to play, he was entered back into the starting lineup. The coach made the call. In this case, I had to deal with it or make a better situation for myself. At this point in my life, there was no better situation so I hung in there. This was the coach's decision, but I did not let this affect my attitude. This is the way I viewed it. I could not change the outcome and any other type of attitude would have been detrimental to me and to my team. Besides, if the coach had not allowed me back onto the squad, after initially being cut, I would not have experienced being a part of a very special team. As a senior, I was part of a very good basketball team that went 30-4. This team was within one game of a national tournament and lost a game, in which it had never trailed, at the buzzer on a half court shot off the glass.

"It ain't over till it's over."
Yogi Berra

Two years after graduating from high school, I had "bulked up" to almost one hundred and fifty-five pounds and was playing the guard position. At this time, I was amazed at the number of guys who had previously played ahead of me on my high school basketball team. Two years later, I had passed most of them by solely because I kept practicing and playing a game I loved, as often as possible.

Thirty years later at a local church picnic, I found out, via the former assistant basketball coach, something I wish I had heard years earlier. The head coach had told him a few years after I had graduated that he felt he had misdiagnosed my talent. It was good to hear, but if only he had recognized it three decades earlier while on the practice floor. I just kept working hard and never thought of quitting the team at any time. The rewards came late in my senior year and throughout the following two seasons at a four year college. My efforts did eventually pay off, just not in the period I would have preferred. A quote from the legendary John Wooden's set of normal expectations probably summed up my particular situation in one sentence.

"Acquire a peace of mind by becoming the best you are capable of becoming."
John Wooden

If an athlete is chosen to be part of a team, he must work hard to improve himself at every practice, as well as in the games. If he works to his full potential, he contributes to the whole team by bringing out the best in all other members. This is what it means to be a TEAM. A single player is part of what should be a cohesive unit and his motives and desires are secondary. A good coach will keep this balance of individual and team. This can be a very difficult task as a coach must not stifle the creativity of the more talented players, but must make these players understand they are not bigger or more important than the TEAM! An excellent example of this occurred at the

University of North Carolina during the Michael Jordan era. Head coach Dean Smith knew he had something special in Jordan right from the start. However, he had to get one of the most talented basketball players ever to "buy into the system" and realize that no individual was greater than the team. In other words, Michael would not be able to display his talents as he might have at another college. John Wooden addressed this subject in *They Call Me Coach*, for he had encountered a similar situation decades earlier with a young player named Lew Alcindor.

A quote Wooden liked to refer to was: *"The main ingredient in stardom is the rest of the team."*

Never let a young athlete get discouraged or give up on himself. He is on the team and is a vital part of the whole. The youngest of athletes must understand this and recognize that no spot in any team pecking order should ever be final. Good practice and game performances will generally be rewarded. One must not sulk if he is at the end of the bench and one must not take things for granted if he is a starter. All players must constantly strive to improve themselves. Tug McGraw helped to rally his New York Mets team to a pennant in 1973 with the battle cry "Ya Gotta Believe." "Ya Gotta Believe" not only in your team, but "Ya Gotta Believe" in yourself, as a person and as an athlete.

Although the preceding paragraphs may seem biographical in nature, it was done so to stress the importance of persistence. Good things may come from failure if you have the proper attitude. These types of situations may occur many times during a child's lifetime, but he must never lose faith!

Nothing in the world can take the place of persistence. Talent will not: Nothing is more common than unsuccessful men with talent. Genius will not: Unrewarded genius is almost a proverb. Education will not: The world is full of educated derelicts. Persistence and determination are omnipotent.

Calvin Coolidge

SPORTSMANSHIP

n(1745): conduct (as fairness, respect for one's opponent, and graciousness in winning and losing) becoming to one participating in a sport.
Merriam-Webster Collegiate Dictionary

As old-fashioned as it may sound my dad's only constant advice was to always DO MY BEST, PLAY HARD, and be a GOOD SPORT. After college, I continued to play in recreational softball leagues until I was 35 and in competitive basketball leagues until I was almost fifty years old. Although I was certainly never overly angelic towards the officials after my collegiate career ended I rarely used profane language and was most concerned the officials assigned to the game took it somewhat seriously. During my youth, high school and four years of college athletics game behavior was NEVER an issue. The coaches took care of this. If you wanted to play, you behaved yourself. Technical fouls or being tossed out of a game was taboo because this would only be the start of the punishment inflicted on a juvenile athlete. After the contest was over the coach, school, and more than likely, the parents would finish the job. It is too bad technical fouls no longer cause the embarrassment they used to create or that many school districts or leagues have no definitive disciplinary policy for any athlete receiving a technical foul.

In one of my first years of coaching, I remember a particular incident during an eight and nine-year old soccer game that I did not handle very well. The opposing coach was running the score up on us and when it reached 10-0, I turned to my assistant coach and said, "If they score one more goal I will be pulling my team off the field." My assistant quickly rebutted and informed me this would not be a proper response, for I would be slipping to the level of the opposing coach. The score remained the same, but I was, should we say *hot* when I got home and could not get this lambasting off my mind. Almost no one likes to get beat by that type of score. I sat down with a glass of milk and my wife asked me what was wrong, as I must have looked a little distraught. I proceeded to explain to her what had happened and then remarked, "And if I ever get the chance to kick that coach's butt (figuratively speaking) all over the field in a future game, I will not hesitate to do so."

"Well, isn't that nice," my wife responded. "That goes against your philosophy regarding youth sports."

"Yeah, yeah, you're right," I said. "And so was my assistant coach. Everyone is correct tonight except me. One more strike and I'm out." (Oh, the BOY in many a competitive man!)

During an athletic contest, it may be difficult for some to keep emotions in check. On that particular evening I am thankful I kept most of my true feelings inside of me until I arrived home, thanks in part to my assistant coach. He probably helped stave off what could have been an embarrassing confrontation. Keeping my feelings in check did not excuse the opposing coach's behavior, but it may have helped to avert an embarrassing situation on that particular evening.

As the years have gone by, I have learned a lot and I should have handled this situation on the field, as opposed to letting the feelings remain bottled up inside of me. I will give you some advice on how to deal with this type of occurrence a little later in this chapter.

Sportsmanship transcends the officials and relates to actions by the opposition, coaches, and even spectators. A player must respect all these parties. The definition at the start of this chapter only referred to the opponent; however, the year of 1745 signifies the first known use of this word in the English language. Sportsmanship also means one should accept the result of a contest in a gracious and polite manner as a winner or, more importantly, as a loser.

"How a man plays the game shows something of his character. How he loses shows all of it."

Unknown

Some programs I have been in contact with leave the "sportsmanship issue" entirely up to the coaches. However, other leagues may distribute bylaws, which might address sportsmanship, to the coaches. The league director may generally ASSUME all coaches will interpret these bylaws "correctly" and the league will function perfectly. There is usually never any follow up and very often, the director of the league is never on site at practices or games to evaluate coaches, players, and officials. Most of the organizational leagues I have been affiliated with have directors who are extremely young and have very limited, if any, experience with youth sports or in dealing with parents. Unfortunately, they are unaware of various situations which can develop regarding parents, coaches, officials, and players. These young directors will soon recognize that just because something is in writing it will not guarantee proper results. Coaches, players, officials, and spectators must continually be observed and monitored with appropriate feedback given as often as possible. Dealing with parents will be one of the most difficult issues a young director may face. As a parent, you may help by approaching any situation you may have to address calmly and rationally. Also, remember to choose the time and place carefully.

A particular episode regarding this occurred in a third and fourth grade basketball league a few years back. As a coach, I received the printed league bylaws and one of the essential ingredients stressed skill development. Additionally, the bylaws stated that team records would not be kept, thus downplaying the importance of winning the game. This meant competition would come secondary to teaching the children the basic skills of the game, the concept of teamwork, and some basic plays. The bylaws also mentioned that if the score differential was twenty points or greater at halftime the scoreboard would be cleared for both teams and started over, if BOTH coaches agreed to it. At this level, I still find it hard to believe that any coach would have a problem with this type of rule. All coaches were cooperative when this type of situation developed save one. This particular coach not only gave the others a rough time about resetting the score, but also seemed to love trying to "kill" the opposition. The league director was nowhere to be found during most of the games. During the season, I had let the director know what was going on, but apparently he never spoke to this coach because things never changed. I can tell you that if the offending coach refused to reset the scoreboard when he played MY team or if he proceeded to run up the score in this third and fourth grade league I would have walked over and spoken to him about it. If he did not adjust (after I had hinted to perhaps NOT fast break so much) I would give him one more chance, but then have to forfeit the game. Why? This coach was embarrassing my team and making a mockery of the game. HE was not following the rules. HE was not respecting the opponent. There is nothing wrong with this approach and as a coach; I would have been in concert with the league bylaws. The icing on the cake occurred when the aforementioned coach proceeded to hand out "first place" trophies, at the end of the year pizza party, to his entire squad in the presence of all the other teams. The league director was not present at this year-end "celebration," but should have been! This coach should have been asked to go off the premises for these types of awards, since they were not sanctioned by the league. All players did get a participatory trophy, which is what this league tried to stress.

Limiting the amount of competition at this age level has great benefits. First, the children must learn the game, before *cutthroat* competition turns them away from it. A team can play to win, but a good coach will know when to *call off the dogs.*

I was startled when a fellow coach in a Catholic varsity basketball league called and asked me how I was able to control my players during a game. This was an adult, in his late forties, just like me. To me that was a stupid question. (Now I know very well in the corporate world or the land of academia it is often said there are no stupid questions, but this was a stupid question. This individual should not have been coaching a team of teenagers if he did not have any ideas about behavior modification.) I explained to him it was quite simple and answered him with a question of my own: "Are your boys there to play basketball?" Naturally, I knew what his answer would be and informed him the one thing a coach has complete control over is each player's time on the court. If a coach controls nothing else, and whether he likes it or not, he does control the amount of playing time for each team member. Oftentimes, this MUST be used as a disciplinary tool. My team rule was that if a player received a technical foul he would be required to sit out four full quarters. A player's time is extremely important to him and limiting the amount of playing time is often a very effective tool for discipline. This does not mean that you may not lose a player on occasion because he may elect to quit rather than take the punishment. However, in a case such as this the player may be doing the coach a favor because he would be placing self over TEAM. My players received two technical fouls over forty-eight games and one was issued because a player swore at himself after he missed a breakaway lay-up. (In a game where our team almost blew a twenty–five point fourth quarter lead and the frustration level was very high.) This was particularly difficult for me to enforce because I did not agree with the referee, but a coach cannot afford to become subjective or you will open a Pandora's Box. Therefore, I had no choice, but to suspend the player for the next game. When I called to tell the parents the specifics, they gave me their full support on the decision. Unfortunately, it does not happen this way all the time. This youngster got his share of discipline at home and all parties understood the consequences of his actions. This was a simple, yet proven method, which worked. However, the coach must enforce the rule or it will not have any "teeth." Enforcing it the first time, was indeed the toughest, but once players saw I was serious, it was only necessary to use it one more time over a four-year period.

A few years earlier I had to suspend a player for one game due to what I felt was unsportsmanlike behavior on the court. The opposing coach heard one of my players utter a racial slur to one of his players. The officials let it slide when, in fact, my player should have been assessed a technical foul. I did not take something like this lightly and proceeded to do some follow up work speaking to the officials, players, as well as the opposing coach. After speaking to all parties, I decided the player had to be suspended for one game. The next morning at work, I got a telephone call from the player's father. He questioned my decision and actually tried to rationalize his son's bad choice by referring to a few incidents where his son's former high school football coach even used racial slurs. I could not believe he headed in this direction, but listened without interruption. Once he said his piece, I said mine, but did not budge regarding my decision. He closed by asking me, "If this were your son would you issue the same punishment?" I assured him it would have been no different. When I repeated this conversation to my wife later that evening, she informed me that it would have been different if it were my son. She believed my son would have been done for the season, so in retrospect perhaps a one game suspension for an incident such as this was not enough.

Good sportsmanship towards the officials, opponents, coaches and spectators should be learned and practiced at an early age and will be important throughout one's athletic career. During any athletic contest, our youth must be taught to keep their emotions under control and to respect the officials' calls. Any youth program, which does not stress this, is missing a vital component. Athletics are not all about the games! The behavior of spectators and players has deteriorated rapidly over the past couple of decades from the youth level, through high school and college, and all the way up to the professional ranks. All athletes and fans in attendance should be accorded a safe environment and it is the responsibility of not only the officials and administrators, but also the coaches to insure this occurs. A one-page flyer handed out to all spectators at a recent high school basketball game I attended summed it up nicely. It read:

SPORTSMANSHIP

LET THE PLAYERS
--- PLAY

LET THE COACHES
--- COACH

LET THE OFFICIALS
--- OFFICIATE

ENJOY THE GAME!

Now that says it all!

Some communities and school districts across the country are finally taking a stand regarding spectator behavior. Some organizations now require parents to attend classes on sportsmanship and ethics. These types of programs should be held on a continuing basis and may eventually have to involve more than just the athlete's parents. For example, if a school district is involved, all students should be required to attend a program regarding sportsmanship and spectator behavior. A California community has actually begun handing out yellow cards to misbehaving spectators. (Similar to soccer penalties.) If a spectator acquires two at any given contest, he is escorted from the premises.

Recently, I volunteered to referee a fifth and sixth grade basketball game and listened to an opposing fan beg for some sort of a foul call every time his son's team was on offense. This particular father was setting a poor example and not being a good sport. Shortly into the second half, during a time out, I very politely asked him (from across the court) if he would take the extra whistle I carried and help me out. All the spectators heard his somber refusal and he was as quiet as a church mouse the rest of the game. The mission was accomplished. It is unfortunate this occurred, but he would not have stopped if I did not ask him for assistance. He got my point. Naturally, we are not all alike and many parents would not be able to do this. However, a little straight forwardness will often stop this obnoxious behavior, but it must be done in a friendly or comical, and not in a threatening manner. (I did not even have an extra whistle, but I knew in advance what his response would be. By his comments, I knew he was not "basketball intelligent" and he was not in shape to run the floor.)

Additionally, on game days parents should not be a distraction to their child from the sideline. This can be an extremely difficult task for some, but remember there is a coach and it is his job to do the constructive criticizing. You do not want to give your child mixed signals. This type of situation could create a lot of confusion. I am not speaking about a spoken word of encouragement here and there, but the constant bombardment of phrases, which may cause a child to search out the parent and make

TAKE THIS, MOM. IF YOU KEEP THIS IN YOUR MOUTH FOR THE WHOLE GAME MAYBE YOU WILL NOT BE EJECTED TODAY.

eye contact in the stands. This is uncalled for and a bad move from all perspectives. Parents must not coach the game from the stands! Occasional encouragement – YES. Constant coaching – NO. As a parent, if you find it difficult to remain somewhat quiet during an event, then sit as far away from the action as you can. Here it will be less difficult to be a distraction. Take a crossword puzzle or a good book to help relieve what may be some excess energy or adrenaline. You may look a little bit foolish, but your child will be happier. Remember it is really the child's game and time to enjoy, not yours.

Last spring at a thirteen and under AAU basketball tournament game in Scranton, Pennsylvania, I saw a father trying to instruct his son from the bleachers under the basket during the game. The kid was trying to play the game, listen to his father, and pay attention to the coach all at the same time. By the end of the game, a very frustrated young man was in tears as his father was still trying to make a few points. At this time, the coach approached the father and politely pointed out that the boy became very confused when his father was shouting to him during the contest. As a player, he was trying to receive instruction from two different sources, which is impossible! The coach of this team deserves a lot of credit. He made his point in a truthful and yet respectful manner. What an embarrassing situation this father created for himself, his son, the coach, and the rest of the team!

This past April, while acting as an official scorer during an AAU basketball game, I had to remind a father next to me that he was not allowed to shout at or "coach" his son from the official scorer's table. I have witnessed this occur quite frequently over the years, but never when I was the official scorer. In another instance, I saw a father, acting as the official timekeeper, evicted from the scorer's table because he was constantly questioning the calls made by one of the officials. This once again created a very embarrassing situation for the home team, their coach and most especially for the son of the father who was "shown to the door." As a parent, if you are involved in some sort of an official capacity whether it is as a timekeeper, scorekeeper, or an official you MUST keep your emotions and bias under control or you should decline any invitations to be involved in any of these capacities.

A good phrase for every spectator to recall when attending any youth sporting event is the ending phrase to a poem I saw on a high school gymnasium wall:

"So please don't curse those boys down there each one his parent's son. And win or lose you see, to us, they're NUMBER ONE."

Also, remember that the officials are somebody's son or daughter, and might even be someone's mother or father. Usually they are putting forth the best effort they can and do not deserve to have a constant barrage of demeaning comments or profanities hailed all over them. An occasional comment or "open your eyes ref" is one thing, but to verbally attack someone personally or bombard with profanity should be grounds for dismissal from the premises. At some point a game official must say, "enough is enough" and ask cooperation from school administrators, security, or a coach to have any obnoxious spectators removed from the premises before the game continues. Once a few evictions occur and the message gets out that the league is serious about promoting good fan behavior, the problem fans will lessen. Unfortunately, this probably needs to happen more often for the offending spectators to get the message.

This past winter I was happy to see one of our local school districts moving in the right direction regarding the issue of sportsmanship. The athletic director of the school was very visible at a varsity basketball contest and circulated throughout the gymnasium as an astute observer of fan behavior. Well, a few students from the visiting school were yelling personal and demeaning comments at one of the opposing players that were way out of line. This *A.D.* sat nearby, listened for a bit, and then approached the guilty students letting them know this was not proper behavior (sportsmanship). He also told them that if it continued they would be asked to leave the contest. I happened to know one of the students involved and ran into him a few days later at a local convenience store. The vital parts of the conversation went something like this.

"Mr. Mohney, why did that guy come up and tell some of my friends what he did at the game on Saturday?"

"Well, Mike, being an athlete yourself you may know it is okay to shout a thing here and there regarding a player or an official and we all know it goes on. However, when you start to use profanity or start to attack players or officials personally it crosses over the line. That was the *A.D.* and he was right to have taken that approach."

"Oh, I see," Mike replied.

I could tell by the look on his face there was some thought process going on inside this teenager's head. I knew he was an athlete at our high school and hoped he would understand. I soon found out by the lack of an argumentative response that he did.

This athletic director deserved to be commended for this type of action. This type of action is what is needed to help get better sportsmanship back into youth sporting events.

When you attend a youth sporting event as a parent, spectator or both strive to:

"Let the game bring out the BEST in you, not the BEaST."
Kurt J. Mohney

RESPECT

In relation to athletics the definition of respect which I like the best is "to recognize the worth, quality, and importance of." Respect must be accorded to the teammates, the opponents, the officials, the coaches, the parents, and the spectators. The facilities, playing surfaces, and the equipment must also be treated with respect. Too often, the second part of this "equation" is overlooked or taken for granted. The upkeep of the facilities and equipment, as well as the maintenance of the playing surfaces requires a good amount of money today. As taxpayers and as parents we are all footing the bill. If proper respect is given, it will maximize the usage of the facilities and equipment alike.

At a very young age, a child must be taught to respect his teammates. It does not mean one has to agree with everything a teammate does or says, but making fun of, belittling, or if not done in a proper manner, even admonishing a teammate is wrong. The coach should be the one to correct a player's actions at the youngest of ages ESPECIALLY during a game. Players need to PLAY, not coach, or officiate for that matter. If teammates do not respect each other, it will be much more difficult to function as a team.

My former high school basketball coach once used a unique way to get his point across to the starting five during my senior year. This unit consisted of me, as well as the only four other seniors on a twelve-man squad. Almost every practice the same two seniors were always bickering and contradicting each other regarding various "court matters." They had little respect for each other. At one practice, the coach had heard enough and asked all five members of the first TEAM to remain after practice. After speaking about the issue of respect and reminding all of us there was only one coach, he proceeded to teach us further.

"Okay," he said, "take off your shirt and exchange it with the teammate standing next to you."

Now I knew what was coming next, but I could hardly bear the thought as I stood there with a sweat-filled shirt in my right hand. (It did not seem fair. Being a skinny runt, I had just turned over a very dry shirt to the heavyset teammate on my left. So goes the lesson on respect and TEAM.)

"Now put it on," the coach exclaimed.

I thought I was going to throw up, but held my breath as I slithered it over my head and let it slide over my small chest. It was definitely cold and wet, but worst of all stunk to high heavens! I would breathe through my mouth, I thought, and this nightmare would be over soon. Our coach had made his point. The lesson was learned, but then:

"Okay, now give me two long *Syracuse sprints*," he screamed.

Now breathing through my mouth would no longer be an option. Now I not only had to wear, but was forced to smell my heavyset teammate's sweat. I thought for sure I would pass out right there in front of everyone.

After we completed this set of sprints, the coach wasted little time before making the next request. "Now it's time for gym short exchange."

I loved this sport, but was not sure I was going to make it through this practice. The slimy, stinky shirt was bad enough! Now I had to search out a different teammate for a short exchange? I hustled to find a less sweaty teammate than my "first exchanger." I wanted to scream, "I get the point! I get the point! I surrender," but never mustered the courage. After we had all slithered into a fellow teammate's gym shorts, the coach proclaimed we would be running two more of his famous sprints. I was beginning to think this experience was a bad dream. (Actually closer to a nightmare.) A few minutes later, we were back at the baseline for our next set of directives. Through all of this, the rest of the team had aligned themselves all around the outside of the gymnasium watching these proceedings. I knew because periodically I could here the laughter coming from the surrounding hallways.

"Now," said the coach, "does everybody get the picture on what it is to respect a teammate and how all of you are in this together? I need an answer from all of you or we will work on exchanging one last piece of gear."

Oh my God. He is kidding, I thought to myself. I probably answered loud enough for the five of us by yelling, "Yes, yes, we get the picture!" I knew I was a goner if we had to exchange jock straps. I could not even stand to guard or bump into someone who was sweaty. The coach chased us out of the gym as all four teammates followed my lead and the guilty two never bickered again. None of us even questioned why all five of us were punished because we knew the message the coach was striving to get across. We were not a good basketball team and not even a mediocre one, but as spoken in the old pirate movies we should be, "all for one, and one for all." We knew the meaning of the word TEAM, although we were not a very good one!

This was a lesson well taught by our coach because as you can see I have never forgotten it. To this day, I will never know if my coach would have made us perform the last exchange if we did not have the correct answer, but I can tell you none of us were worse for wear. None of our parents ever confronted the coach because we deserved it. This was part of our education too! As an athlete, there are times one must suck it up and move on. If a lesson needs to be taught, or a point needs to be made, sometimes a more dramatic course of action is necessary. One episode, one phrase, or one shouting spell should not turn an athlete away and oftentimes the parents should simply support the coach. If a child is not constantly berated, or mentally or physically abused there is generally no need for concern. Your young athlete's "career" will not always be filled with pleasurable occurrences.

Everyone must also remember to respect the playing surfaces. Do not walk across gymnasium floors in wet or dirty shoes when a contest is taking place. You will jeopardize the safety of the contestants and the officials if they slip on a wet spot or a patch of dirt. A few years back during a local high school basketball game, I actually saw an official run **around** a spectator who was ten feet inside the court. This "spectator" was strutting next to his girlfriend with a set of headphones on, clueless to the dangerous situation he was creating for the players and officials (as well as himself and his girlfriend). In this instance, the individual should have been escorted out of the gym because he placed numerous parties at risk. This was solely a result of ignorance and should not have been tolerated. It went virtually unnoticed because the athletic director was nowhere to be found and the officials did not notify the security staff about the happening.

Do not ride bicycles or four wheelers across outdoor fields used for athletic events and do not use any field under extreme weather conditions that could damage the surface for many months ahead. Teach team members to pickup all litter near benches, in dugouts and around bleachers and spectator areas when an event has concluded, even if the garbage does not belong to them. (A warning: "But it isn't mine" will be a favorite line of many young athletes.) Also, treat all the equipment issued to the team, by whatever organization, with respect. Do not walk over bat handles, leave equipment out in the rain or snow, hang onto basketball rims, etc. etc. Some of the things I have mentioned may seem ridiculous to mention, but I have seen every one of them occur and sometimes wonder if our youth are really getting the proper message. Are they being held accountable when things are damaged or "stolen"? If they are not held accountable, they will never get the message.

John Affleck, my former college basketball coach at Binghamton University, used to instruct the players to share the secrets of some of our best skills with fellow teammates. We were asked to help educate our teammates on how we performed a particular move or what type of drills we used to perfect it. By sharing one is not only respecting and helping a teammate, but also enhancing one's own development. How? My teammate became more familiar with my thought process and physical moves, perhaps making it a little easier to guard me during practice sessions. Therefore, I was forced to develop new techniques if I was to be "on top of my game " during intersquad scrimmages. The coach consistently stressed that when we helped each other we were in essence helping ourselves. Isn't this another version of what is called the Golden Rule? ("Do unto others as you would have them do unto you.")

"Respect is what we owe; love is what we give."
                                        Philip James Bailey

HUMILITY

Humility is defined in the Merriam-Webster Dictionary as "the quality or state of being humble." To gain further insight one must research further and find out that the word humble is defined as "not proud or haughty or arrogant or assertive." Although any athlete must ascertain a certain degree of confidence and pride, it should be kept under control and be balanced with a dose of humility. The author C.S. Lewis said, "Pride is the complete anti-God state of mind." I do not completely agree with this statement because one must take a certain degree of pride in his work. Taking pride in one's work helps one to battle through life's daily struggles. Lewis would not have been a successful author if he had no pride in his work as an author. As with many other things in life, the scale must be balanced with proper weights of pride and humility.

Every athlete is familiar with the person who walks in the gymnasium with the Hollywood sneakers, jewelry, and a flashy uniform to match. Oftentimes, the "hot shot's" jersey will show the name of a great college or professional player. Well, everybody nearby usually checks him out because he is calling a lot of attention to himself, looking like a walking billboard. Then when he steps on the court he razzle-dazzles everyone with a few quick dribbling drills to warm up, but when play begins everyone may quickly find out he can't throw the ball into the Atlantic Ocean, let alone make a basket. His lack of interest in playing defense may also allow him to "get lit up like a Christmas tree" by an opponent. Any athlete will quickly recognize this type of individual. Just because a guy may dress the part and TRY to act it means nothing. The better athlete does not need to draw any extra attention. A good player will get everyone's attention soon enough by the way he plays the game. It is up to any athlete to develop character, not be a character. The following quote specifically referenced politics, but may also be applied to anticipated athletic performance.

"It is best to under promise and over deliver."
Rudolph Guliani

An athlete should not call attention to himself with his dress, talk, or actions. Let the way one "plays the game" do the talking!

I could have addressed showmanship in the chapter on sportsmanship, but I felt it was a better fit when speaking about humility. Many professional athletes often set poor examples when it comes to celebrating a routine move or score. The high fives and dancing after a quarterback sack, the chest bumping after a home run, or the fist pumping after a dunk are such examples. This is showmanship and has no place in youth sports. All of these are parts of the game and part of the professional athlete's job. Should a mechanic go out and do a cartwheel in the street after performing an oil change? Should a waiter go back into the kitchen to give the chef a high five and a few chest bumps after he serves a meal? Maybe a corporate accountant should run around the parking lot yelling and pumping his fist in the air every time he closes the monthly books. They are just doing their jobs, but outbursts such as these would look foolish! Supposedly, these "professionals" are just doing their jobs, but you would not know it the way they carry on. The thing I hate the most at all levels of basketball is the hand slapping which occurs after a "made" free throw. For

Pete's sake that why it's called a FREE throw. A comedian once remarked after witnessing two NBA players slap hands with a teammate after he has missed a free throw: "He doesn't need a slap on the hands. He deserves a slap in the face." This may be extreme, but he made his point. The only distractions should be the fans. One does not need a teammate interrupting his concentration just for making a free throw. (I am not speaking about the free throw with seconds to go in the game when the pressure is REALLY on.) Each free throw is one among many, as is every play during a game. Michael Jordan did not celebrate every play or basket, for he knew the goal was to win the game. Then, when that goal was accomplished, he may have thrust his fist toward the sky knowing that his TEAM had won the game. The *showboating* that occurs today in professional sports has no place in the amateur leagues of this country. Do not let any part of these types of "professional" actions permeate any part of your youth athletic leagues. All athletes on the field or the floor at a given time are there for a common purpose and are part of a team. Do not allow the team's reputation to suffer due to one or two athletes who do not know how to control themselves. (Remember once again, there is no "I" in team.)

Again, the word balance comes into play. Parents and players should try to keep their emotions in check by not getting too high after a win or too low after a loss. After all, even most games at the high school level are just league games albeit perhaps important, but not a league championship and certainly not a matter of life and death. Winning is only part of the game and must be kept in a proper perspective. Try taking things in stride and everyone's health will be the better for it. The sun will always come up the next day. Remember it is very important for a parent to teach a young athlete how to win and how to lose.

Parents should try to remain somewhat humble about a child's achievements in the athletic arena. As parents we should be proud of each child's accomplishments, but must also keep in mind how quickly things may change due to various circumstances we have no control over. We must all be prepared to take the good along with the bad and remember: "One is only as good as his last game." I like to remind my youngest son that I like the opposite of this phrase: "One is only as bad as his last game." After a bad performance, I could not wait for the next game day to arrive to try to redeem myself for a prior game's dour actions! An athlete should never view any game performance as if it were his last. Many opportunities will lie ahead!

Above all, refrain from telling someone you are counting on your young athlete to make it to the professional ranks and help contribute to your "lousy pension plan" or to buy you a house on Nantucket Island. According to the National Center for Educational Statistics, less than 1% of all children who participate in organized sports will qualify for an athletic scholarship. This statistic may help a parent to keep athletics in proper perspective. By the time your child graduates from high school, chances are his athletic skills will be exactly average. He probably will not be headed for the professional sports level, nor will he be a computer geek or headed for Oxford.

If your son or daughter is above average, the parents must try to remain humble. Without knowing it, some statements you may make will help to isolate people from you and many will be laughing behind your back. God has given you the gift of a healthy child and if he is blessed with the ability to excel in whatever endeavor(s) he chooses, many should be very thankful.

THE COACHES

At the early age levels, the most important attribute a coach must possess is common sense and a mentality that recognizes "winning" should be second nature. Many adult coaches are extremely dedicated to youth sports. These individuals deserve high praise for the time they devote to such an admirable cause. All coaches should be aware of young children's differences and adapt as needed to make the PLAYING experience a positive one.

IF THIS IS HOW THEY ACT WHEN THEY DON'T WIN YOU MUST BE DOING SOMETHING RIGHT!

At the youngest of ages, all children must be assured of a fair amount of playing time. There must also be a de-emphasis on winning. It may be at times ironic to use the term "playing time" because of the way some of the youth coaches treat their players and the opposition during any given contest. I am sure many of the young players might not consider it "play." Oftentimes, there may be too much pressure being put on the participants, from various fronts, to consider it "play."

Many coaches will lack some elementary knowledge when dealing with children. At the youngest of age levels, a coach must not have a "win at all costs mentality." A basic knowledge of the game and its rules should be a main ingredient. The knowledge of what drill is necessary to teach a particular skill is also essential. A coach should not just toss a soccer ball onto the field or a basketball on the court and shout, "let's scrimmage." This type of approach will not benefit the children. Well-organized, repetitive, fast moving drills are needed for a young athlete's development. If a coach cannot run a controlled practice, it will not be the proper environment for your child to learn the sport. Never let a coach play your child if he is injured, sick, or just plain "does not feel like playing." Usually the "do not feel like playing" issue will have some underlying themes, which you as a parent, must open up for discussion and get to the real "reason." If this occurs, it is extremely important that you explore it soon as it could prove vital to your child's future development.

At the youngest of ages, a coach should not *pigeonhole* a child to a particular position. For example, if a child is left-handed he should not be labeled a first baseman for life. Just because he is heavy, should not make him a fullback forever, or because he is tall, he should not be branded a center for eternity. Kids should get to experience different positions, if they desire. Sometimes a little persuasion is necessary and in the end, the child will benefit from this experience.

Remember too, a coach is not God and accidents may happen. I thought that I always had a good handle on my youth practices and yet an accident occurred during a minor-league baseball practice with primarily nine- and ten-year-old boys. After explaining and reviewing a baseball throwing and catching line drill we were about to use I concluded by saying,

"And remember when you are in line DO NOT stand directly behind the person receiving the throw." Then, what I now refer to as the "Trevor Cubed" incident happened:

"Trevor A" (the biggest kid and wildest thrower on the team), threw a bullet to "Trevor B" (the shortest kid on the team) standing about thirty feet away. The ball sailed over the head of "Trevor B" and struck an unsuspecting, daydreaming "Trevor C" (who happened to be my kid) square in the privates. He fell to the ground like a sack of potatoes. I had explained the drill thoroughly and always preached the danger of a bat and ball, oftentimes referring to them as weapons, and yet this still occurred. This is humorous years later, but at the time was a very serious accident.

If "cuts" are required, the coach owes every contestant who failed to make the team an explanation. This comes with the territory, but I am truly surprised this topic is not covered in any of the "educational" coaching courses I have previewed or been involved with over the years. These courses seem to review all the first aid issues and how to deal with players once they make the team, but fail to instruct "wannabee" coaches how to deal with candidates who have not met their grade. The lists posted on the door or on a gymnasium wall are primitive and cold. ("A wimpy way" as one parent once remarked.) The "if you do not get a telephone call by this time on Sunday night" is a copout. Any good coach should be able to call the youngster aside and have a brief conversation explaining why he did not make the team.

A coach should always encourage a child never to give up, but to work on improving his skills and try out for the team again in the future without EVER giving any candidate the false hope the following year's result might be different. I remember the spring of my eldest son's tenth birthday. He was trying out for the local little league team and my wife and I had only mediocre hopes of him making it. When the last day of tryouts had ended, my son arrived at our side door somewhat disappointed, but not in tears, as I had been almost thirty-five years earlier on at least three different occasions. "I didn't make it, but the coach said I probably will next year," he said. I can honestly say he did not make it "fair and square" and the coach should NOT have issued such a statement giving what seemed almost like a promise. The coach should have told him what he needed to work on and to "give it another shot" the following spring. My son was "on the fence" to begin with and had only a slight chance of making the team.

If someone wishes to coach, he must learn to deliver the bad news as truthfully as the good news. It is always easier to preach the good news, but the bad news must also be communicated in a compassionate, truthful, and helpful way. As difficult as it may be, a coach must communicate honestly to the children who fail to make the squad. A handwritten sheet or checklist of what could be improved upon is a nice touch. This approach has worked wonderfully for me, but I must admit it takes some preparation and at times fortitude to maintain one's composure. On at least a couple of occasions, I fought back tears. However, all contestants are deserving of this type of audience with the coach. I once had to cut an eleventh grader from a basketball team, but the next year he tried out again, made it and to this day has remained one of my favorite players. This former player is now in graduate school preparing for a career in sport's management. This particular individual did not look at making the team as an end, but as a process. He was persistent and for him it paid off. He learned certain things from being a member of an athletic team, which will benefit him throughout life. When participating in athletics one need not be the star of a team to gain benefits that will last a lifetime.

As in the business world, not all is fair and most decisions involve subjective judgment. A coach should always have a reason and explanation for his actions. Any good coach will announce ALL spots are available during the tryout sessions. A prior year player should never be guaranteed a spot the following year. If a player has the proper talents, he will surely earn a position during the tryout session.

It is also imperative for a coach to recognize the last five players on the bench are at least as important as the starters. It is much easier for those players getting game time to show up day in and day out at practice than it is for the guys at the end of the bench. Believe me, as I was in both positions in grade school, high school and in college. The players at the end of the bench are needed so practices can be run and the starters can be pushed to over achieve and be ready for game day. It is easier to attend daily practices if you feel you are contributing on game day. It takes a very good attitude to attend practice day after day, as a member of the second or third team, when you realize you may never make it off the bench during the next game. Additionally, a coach must evaluate a player's attitude, as well as his work ethic. If a player will only see a marginal amount of P. T., the coach should think about how this player might react to sitting on the bench game after game. If the player is a complainer and has lousy practice habits, it would be better for the coach to choose someone else. The player chosen might have less talent, but would be better for team unity.

Additionally, a coach must always be aware of the team chemistry and be sure all teammates respect one another. There should be no tolerance for any team member to constantly belittle or make fun of another. One must remember that occasional bickering and arguments will occur, but these must soon be forgotten and can often be used as a learning experience. A parent should remember that even in the best of families many disagreements and arguments do occur. If no resentment is harbored and something is learned, the result may often be very beneficial. Various types of team chemistry are present in sports. I am reminded of two very different championship baseball teams. The 1979 Pittsburgh Pirates had the theme song "We Are Family" because of a team bond on and off the field. The Oakland Athletics, of the early 1970s, often had fights in the clubhouse. Both of the clubs won World Series titles with extremely different team chemistries. Everyone on every team will not always like each other. This is important to remember.

I once witnessed a basketball game in which my oldest son was the only one on the team who failed to get into a game that was a blowout. I said nothing during or after the contest, but gave the coach a call the next day. He apologized, admitted it was his fault, and said that he would not let it happen again. I appreciated this response, but it was imperative to have addressed this type of situation. A coach must be aware of all players on the bench, especially at the end of a game where the outcome has already been decided. ALL players deserve playing time during the last few minutes of a game when its outcome is no longer in doubt.

Generally, a school sanctioned athletic program hires coaches who have a decent knowledge of the sport they will coach. (This may not always be the case if a district has few applicants for the job.) However, this is very often not the situation with various community or service organization sports. These organizations may take the first individual who volunteers, regardless of his past experience or knowledge of the sport. I am not suggesting that every parent coach have a

Ph.D. in psychology or psychiatry. Very few community organizations I have ever been affiliated with or am aware of even require the coaches to attend coaching seminars or clinics. Many get little or no training and may struggle when it comes to coaching such diverse lots of fledgling athletes. A few training programs for coaches presently exist, but they are minimal. Most of these programs probably do not address the psychological issues in any depth, but are probably worthy on other fronts. At a minimum, a coaching clinic should include presentations on basic coaching techniques, dealing with discipline problems and parents, basic first aid skills and perhaps a separate clinic on CPR training and defibrillator use. If such clinics are available, volunteer coaches should be required to attend.

As a parent, if you feel you could contribute to enhancing the coach's knowledge, offer your services to help at a practice or two. Many coaches will resent the offer, so do not be disappointed if this occurs. If a coach appears to be open to suggestions, you could also make some printed material available to him regarding the rules of the game or various drills to improve a player's skills. The season will probably be a success if the coach is fair to the children, has control, runs a decent amount of skill drills, and conducts himself in an adult-like manner. If he does not meet some of these criteria, you may be better off placing your young athlete in another situation.

A coach should also have scheduled practice times and must not use the practice time solely to *scrimmage*. The purpose of practices should be to learn the basic skills of the game, as well as various "plays" if it is a team sport. If a coach has two or three practices before the games begin and none thereafter, the situation will prove detrimental. Practices should also be used to review game play and make adjustments and improvements, as needed. If a coach always wants to scrimmage, your child is being done a disservice. Scrimmages and games are not where players improve. Improvement occurs at practice with the repetition of various skill drills, as well as repeatedly reviewing team plays. Skill drills can be made fun even with plenty of repetition built in. Children and parents alike should become familiar with some of the individual drills to use them away from the formal practice time. This is how a child can improve existing skills, as well as develop new ones. If a coach appears to "be in it only for the games" and has infrequent practice sessions the situation should be addressed. Many children will often enjoy the practice sessions more than the organized games and it is here where the learning should be taking place. Controlled scrimmages can be beneficial and on occasion can be used as a reward if a good practice session has ensued.

Always recognize no two coaching styles will be alike and it may be difficult to find the perfect fit for your child. At the younger age levels, it is important for the coach to be a good disciplinarian, as well as a clear communicator who knows something about the sport. You and your child must also recognize the coach is the boss. No one is forcing your child to be a part of the program, so if you do not like the coach or his philosophy you must search out a better fit. As the child matures, and YOU do for that matter, you may recognize distinct differences in coaching styles. One of my best coaches did a few things I was not particularly fond of and frankly many players and parents alike thought he was losing his mind at times. Before a number of varsity basketball games, when our defense was suffering greatly, we ran a "special" pre-game warm-up drill. Each player had to stand in a good defensive posture and let an opposing teammate run into him, not once, but twice to simulate an offensive charge. My feeling was it was bad enough getting run over by an opposing player during a game, why risk getting hurt in warm-ups? Naturally, in those days, no one spoke up, but I thought he was going nuts. (My personal feeling was that he was influenced by Bobby Knight's philosophy on defense at a team camp we attended over the summer.) Then at halftime of every home junior varsity game, which preceded the varsity contest, our fully uniformed squad would have to waltz over to the connected junior high gymnasium to practice shooting free throws. Well, I liked watching my friends on the junior varsity play and was an 85% free throw shooter. I thought, "What good is this doing me? Take the players who throw the missiles and cinder blocks up at the rim. They're the ones who need the practice." However, it was a team game and thirty years ago, most players never dreamed of contradicting an elder, "all-knowing" coach. I went along with it for I did not want to "lose my situation." Many coaches will do some crazy things, but most will have the best interest of the kids in mind.

Remember that all coaches will have different motivational styles. Do not immediately become critical of a coach because he is a "yeller," "bumper," or "pacer." As individuals, we are all different and so are coaches. Their methods of instruction may be vastly different. Oftentimes, a coach may employ a few styles because if at first you do not succeed try and try again, but the next time trying something different may be necessary. The coach may be a "yeller," but do not let that bother you. Chances are he is not getting personal or abusive with your child and is only trying to get his attention to make a point. During many athletic contests, a coach will not be heard unless he raises his voice. I once saw a coach's sweatshirt that read, "I yell because I care." Keep this phrase in mind when a coach is "barking" at one of your offspring. He may have only been trying to get your child's attention, or perhaps he was condemning a particular action he felt was inappropriate. Very often, a coach will point to his head and lip sync the word "THINK" if a player has done something wrong. No one should take this personally. Even the best of players must be reminded to "THINK" on occasion. If the yelling is inappropriate and includes the belittling or embarrassing of your young athlete, you have every right as a parent to speak up. Remember to do this at an appropriate time and in an appropriate manner, as discussed earlier in this book.

If the coach is a "pacer," he is probably the "nervous Nellie" type who needs to prance up and down the sidelines like a protective mother hen. It will be to the coach's benefit if he is also a "yeller" because his pacing distance will be somewhat minimized. It will not be necessary to traverse a great distance to make sure he is heard.

A "bumper" coach will be seen nose to nose with a player on many occasions, explaining a broken play or mistake made. Although there is usually no need for concern, it would be beneficial for the players if the coach is a non-smoker and has good oral hygiene. With this type of coach, a player may often try to distance himself, but the coach will continue to creep closer. It is generally hopeless for a player to establish the distance for a "normal" conversation. This type of coach may often place his finger on a player's head, shoulder, or knee to be sure the player is paying attention. Some coaches just like a little more contact with the players to be sure they have a player's undivided attention.

If you are fortunate to garner a coach without a child on the team AND with some basic knowledge about working with children and the sport itself, consider yourself blessed. In this case, parental bias will never be an issue and very often, the experience will be a good one. My youngest two sons played on a little league team, coached by a "twenty-five ish" young man, and had three great seasons of baseball. Although one of my boys did not play that often, it did not concern me. I knew the coach was fair and Trevor always enjoyed going to practice, as well as the games. The friendship and camaraderie meant a lot to him and so did that uniform! In addition, he always enjoyed the concession stand and going out with the team for pizza or ice cream after the game. Trevor's priorities were in order – for HIM! He participated and enjoyed it.

Remember too that even the best of coaches are still human. Mistakes will be made and a coach may not have a solution or answer for every situation or question that arises. Here is an example of what I mean:

Imagine that your child's team is playing in a very tight basketball game. It is a very close and hard fought contest and to the coaches and spectators, all appears normal. Well, during a time out the best offensive player tells his coach that the opposing player guarding him is at times playing a little rough and dirty. However, he is sly enough to hide it from the official. Of course, the correct answer to the young athlete would be to have good self-control, ignore it, walk away, and not retaliate. These types of personal qualities should be admired. However, on the athletic field? Is this really how an athlete should respond? At the youngest of ages, the game official(s) and opposing coach need to be informed of what is going on. After a brief period of observation, it may become necessary for an official and or the opposing coach to let the player know that behavior such as this is unbecoming of a young athlete. As a young athlete matures, it may often be extremely difficult for coaches to instruct or advise an athlete regarding a matter such as this one. Certain characteristics that we admire in people such as compassion, gentleness and kindness are diametrically opposed to the characteristics of a successful athlete like aggressiveness, intensity and a great deal of confidence. (That at times may border on cockiness.) A coach, or parent for that matter, may never have the proper answer for everything that takes place on the athletic field. It is best to let a cool head prevail when responding to a question such as this, especially if you do not have something constructive to say to the child. Under no circumstances should you tell him to go out and retaliate by taking on the "eye for an eye, tooth for a tooth" mentality. As your athlete matures, he will figure out ways to handle unique situations that develop via his own experiences or by speaking to former and fellow athletes. Very often, the individual in the athletic environment versus the same individual in the normal daily environment has distinctly different personalities. For an athlete to become a different individual *between the lines* is nothing new. He may be a pit bull on the basketball court and a collie in the classroom.

Any good coach will recognize who the most important player on the team is for each parent. The correct answer is, of course, your own child. It is imperative for the coach to treat each child fairly and every parent with respect. Parents, in return, must recognize that many coaches are volunteers and paid coaches usually get minimal stipends. To put it bluntly, the coaches are not in it for the money and they too deserve proper respect. The reason most coaches are involved is that they love the sport and enjoy working with children, but not necessarily in that order.

Coaches at any level should be very concerned about the level of effort the players are putting forth in practice, as well as in the game. If a team is well prepared and putting forth a good effort the score will take care of itself. A coach must be concerned with how his team responds in game situations. In almost four decades of coaching, the former UCLA basketball coach, John Wooden, never used the word "win" when addressing his players. He only asked them to put forth their best effort at ALL times. He was striving to get a perfect team performance, which he realized would never be attained. He must have been doing something right to win ten NCAA national basketball titles!

Perhaps the most important thing any coach could teach his players is to be humble in victory and courageous in defeat. There will always be winners and losers. This lesson, well taught, will go a long way in life.

As a parent always remember to tell the coach "thank you." Many parents do not recognize the great deal of time and effort it takes to coach a team, especially if the coach is doing it in a conscientious manner. Anyone who has ever coached a team knows the effort involved. There have been far fewer parents who have told me "thank you," over the years, compared to those who have said nothing. Please try not to fall into the latter category.

WHAT ARE SOME ADULTS THINKING?

Many times, I hear the phrase: "He's reliving his youth" or "He's a frustrated jock ." Over the past four decades, I have seen some very good former athletes do things that are uncalled for and I have seen frustrated *jocks* do the same. These "performances" occurred while coaching and instructing our youth about sport! I have seen all types of coaches run up the score when it could have been controlled and I have seen many adults treat referees and opposing players (at YOUTH sporting events) with such disrespect it sickened me. I witnessed a seventh grade basketball game several years ago where two coaches yelled and complained for the entire half. My child was not even playing in the game, but I attended because I knew a few of the competitors. (I also knew both coaches.) It was not pleasurable at all and I was embarrassed to be a member of the crowd. It was a very bad scene! I have no idea why the paid officials put up with this type of behavior, as they had every right to issue a technical foul or even to expel the coaches from the gymnasium for behavior unbecoming of a coach.

Unfortunately, our society is not void of confrontational situations and at times, parents MUST take a stand for what is right. If this must be done, a parent must be sure to do it in a proper manner. My oldest son once said, "There is nothing more uncomfortable for a child than to see a parent in an argument or confrontation." I never looked at this from a young child's perspective, but I can readily see how a youngster could feel. More often than not, the participating youngsters know what is going on and what is right. Why can't the adults understand? These sporting events aren't college or professional. These are K – I – D – S. How are we preparing the next generation for participating in and viewing athletic events? In some regards, not very well, I am afraid.

I still do not understand how coaches, at any level can conscientiously run up the score on an opponent, but at the lowest age levels, it is inexcusable. If the two contestants are separated by 50 points, 20 runs or 15 goals a couple of questions must be asked of the "winning" coach:

1. As a youth coach, is HE doing his best to control the score and not make a mockery of the game?

2. Has HE ever been on a team that took a devastating loss? (The answer to this question had better be "no." Any coach who is well schooled in athletics should know how humiliating it can be and would work with his players to control the score, which can be done in numerous ways! See below.)

Then invite this coach over to the losing team's bench and ask your players what type of emotions they are feeling at this time. I am sure embarrassment, frustration, sorrow, and perhaps even anger will be at the top of their list. If by this time, a coach fails to get the message it is a lost cause and he should not be a member of any youth coaching fraternity.

Keep in mind the above questions do not have to be raised during the particular sporting event. Perhaps at the conclusion of the game it would be most appropriate. However, if the situation justifies, a quarter or halftime break might allow you to speak to one of the coaches in private. All leagues should have a rule's committee and bylaws that address such issues as, "what to do in the event of a lopsided score." (A definition of what constitutes a "lopsided score" must be agreed upon, as well as what could be done to control it, or when the game would be called if the "winning" coach could not adhere to the rules. These rules must be VERY specific and properly communicated to both coaches and parents.)

When on the "up side" of a lopsided score I have heard coaches say things such as, "I had a minimal amount of players and I kept my weakest team on the floor at all times." This is not a valid response. There are specific ways to control the score so players at the youngest age brackets will not feel humiliated. Even if a coach happened to be saddled with the minimum amount of players, did he try any of the following?

Ask the players to make a designated number of passes, when on offense, to slow the game down?

Rotate his better players to defense and poorer players to offense to limit the scoring?

Play "station to station baseball?" (Disallow base stealing, as well as stretching singles into doubles to minimize the amount of runs scored.)

Work on a football team's passing game if the running game has been devastating to the opposition, or vice versa.

A coach can employ various methods to prevent "running up the score." I have used most of the above at one time or another, even at the advanced levels where high school athletes were involved and they all worked. I always explained my rationale and asked my teams the simple question:

"How would you feel right now if you were on the other team?"

I never got static from any team I have coached between the fourth and the twelfth grade regarding "controlling" this type of game situation. All players bought in to whatever my proposal happened to be and proceeded to do exactly as I had asked. This merely emphasizes the fact that no one wants to be part of a losing team, which is being humiliated, at any level. I had asked my teams to put themselves in one of the player's positions on the other team and see how they would feel. Apparently, it was not a difficult thing for any of my young athletes to visualize. Additionally, I never felt negative repercussions from any of the parents. After each of these types of games, I always made it a point to tell the team how proud I was for their understanding and cooperation. Although it might have been an extremely difficult thing for the more competitive athletes to do, it was the right thing to do.

A few years back during a teener (ages 13-16) baseball game the opposing team had no experienced catcher and inserted a thirteen-year-old "rookie" behind the plate. Our team had busted out to an early 5-0 lead and I informed everyone sitting in our dugout there would no longer be any base stealing. However, a runner could advance on a passed ball. (If I did not allow this to occur, this too, I felt, would be a mockery of the game.) I got a questionable look from one of my older players and asked him how he would have felt if he were in this young player's position. Enough said, as he was very respectful and got my point. I concluded by stating that if we gave up some runs and the game got close stealing would again become an option.

Does it make a team more successful when they pulverize and embarrass their opposition? I do not believe so. Vince Lombardi, the legendary hall of fame football coach, recognized this type of situation early in his career as an assistant coach at West Point. Lombardi knew there were values in team sports, but there were questions as to where to draw the line between lambasting an opponent versus the need to excel. All coaches should do serious thinking and soul searching regarding this paradox. The answer to this is not black or white, but gray. This is a delicate issue and needs to be given much thought. How each youth coach handles an issue such as this is generally up to his own discretion, but at the youngest of ages the answer should be very clear. Young athletes must not be made to feel embarrassed or humiliated as it may turn them away from athletics at a very young age.

One summer during a teener league game the pitcher for my team made a decision to issue an intentional walk to the opposing team's cleanup hitter with first base open. Our team ended up winning the game, but before game two of a scheduled doubleheader the father of the player to whom we issued the intentional pass, proceeded to escort his son off the field. He took the young athlete home because he was upset about the intentional walk. This was after he had paid a trip INTO our team's dugout to express his displeasure. A parent of a player on the opposing team also heard him say, "I would like to punch that coach's lights out." (THAT coach being ME.) These are two great examples of parental behavior. He "took his ball and went home" because he essentially did not get his way and he physically threatened a coach. What was this parent thinking? I can deal with being threatened because I happened to know the individual, but let us ask ourselves the question: "What if this happened between two people who did not know each other?" This may have escalated into something bigger. This out of control parent is also involved in coaching youth in our area, from the very young all the way up to the high school level. This type of stuff happens and I cannot give any surefire measures to halt it. However, with the way our society is progressing it would probably be a good idea for the various youth clubs and community associations to issue handbooks or provide courses for parents regarding proper behavior. Many of the recreational and community groups must make a better effort in getting to know the types of individuals who are enlisting to coach their children. If a parent steps over the line, with unsportsmanlike behavior, he should be removed from the coaching ranks or be asked not to attend future games. This, however, would be difficult to enforce unless someone has the courage and authority to put the regulations into action. If a parent did not abide by the rule of the governing body, the unfortunate extreme would be to banish the child from league play. I do feel that too often everyone looks the other way and forgets about various situations that must be addressed to prevent future incidents. What may end up happening, due to such occurrences, is that various entities and functions may cease to exist due to all the parental MISbehavior. It will no longer be worth the hassle for the organizers and administrators who are very often volunteers. The benefit to our youth may no longer outweigh the risks. An injustice such as the elimination of many youth sports programs would occur due to parental misbehavior! If this occurred, the generations of tomorrow would miss many of the benefits youth sports provide.

One community in New Jersey has built a four feet deep dry concrete moat just outside the first and third base fences of a little league field. It was constructed to reduce the size of the sideline parents; thus making the parents seem far less

SURE THEY LOOK SILLY, BUT IT'S ALOT BETTER THAN IT USED TO BE.

threatening to their children. This type of occurrence should send the parents a strong message. I hope that the parents are not oblivious to the rational behind this type of construction project. Why is something like this even necessary? Is this how far our country has digressed on the youth sports scene? If some of the parents and spectators still "don't get it," the league administrators should provide a very thorough explanation on the purpose of the moats. The next step may be to ban all spectators from attending the event. When speaking of youth sports it is sad to believe we have digressed to such a state.

I must also warn parents involved with youth athletics about the numerous stories, tales, and outright lies you may hear over the years. You must be prepared to deal with these and try to sort out the fact from fiction, if it is necessary to do so. Also, remember the stories will become embellished and exaggerated as a person ages. It is just human nature. Many coaches will tout their own past athletic prowess and educational background as if this really matters to team members or the parents. Over the years, I have heard it all in my community. One local instructor has children believing he played Division I basketball and I know he never played college basketball at any level. A former coach of a local college team once told a similar story. Another favorite saying is, "I did not play because I did not get along with the coach," which may equate to, "I didn't play because I did not love the sport or because I just wasn't good enough."

A coach may also tell your child, "I was scouted by or had a tryout with the Tuscaloosa Tugboats or some professional team." Well, just remember many high school and college athletes can say they were scouted at one time or another because scouts are all over the place. They may be at a game to see a highly prized prospect, but are witnessing ALL the players. If another athlete has a stellar game, the chances are he will be recognized. In regards to tryouts, oftentimes a candidate may not even need an invitation. Many open tryouts are held for various sports. (In the 1970s the Kansas City Royals held many free and open tryouts for candidates throughout the country.) You must take stories like these with a *grain of salt*. You may soon recognize if the statements are true by how much of the game a coach successfully imparts to your youngster. How he and his team react to certain game situations may also give you a clue.

None of this should matter, but some adults may be lying and the children will eventually find out and lose respect for them. Why would a child believe anything this adult taught them after someone has lied about their past? I did not tell my youngest son the truth about one of these individuals because I wanted him to respect this person as a coach. However, in a few years I will explain to him that what these men said was wrong. These are not embellishments. They are lies.

Even if a coach was a stellar athlete, but has no control over the children at practices and does not spend time on drills, a parent should be wary. On the other hand, a coach may have been a very mediocre athlete, but is a great teacher who has spent a lot of time studying the game. Oftentimes, a more gifted athlete might have done many things due to God-given ability and may not be able to convey certain techniques or skills very well to our youth. Coaching ability is a tough thing to predict. Just remember as far as coaches are concerned: "Past (athletic) performance does not guarantee future (coaching) results." Playing and coaching are two different ballgames. However, the evaluation of a coach should not be much different from a parent's evaluation of a teacher. Coaching is essentially an extension of the classroom in many regards. Parents must observe their child's coach and see if he is a positive or negative

107

role model. If the coach is deemed a bad influence and you refuse to address the situation, you may regret your lack of action. If you decide to confront the coach regarding a particular situation and he refuses to change, your only choices are to speak to the league director or remove your child from the team. If you remove your child from the team, it is imperative to explain to the coach and league director just why you have taken this action. The proper authorities must be notified and perhaps actions will be taken to improve things in the future. If you remain silent, expect nothing to change for the better. Sometimes a proper confrontation and ensuing discussion is a necessity to help to improve the athletic program as a whole.

PARTING SHOTS

Don't let your child talk you into letting him be a "fashion statement" for his sport at a young age or it will only get worse as he gets older. In the corporate world, "clothes may make the man," but with athletics it is much to the contrary. A player should have well-conditioned and good looking and fitting equipment, but it need not be top shelf or the latest thing on the store racks. I know at times it will be a battle, but you should go for middle of the road price at a young age or you can "break the bank." I may come across as being a little harsh because when it comes to clothing I am not what one would call the "aisle of style," but I believe most parents will know where I am coming from regarding an athlete's apparel.

My first baseball glove was a well-worn first baseman's mitt given to me by an uncle. The mitt was at least ten seasons old before I got my little hand into it. It had a huge web compared to what most of my friends had on their expensive new gloves and due to my glove's uniqueness, it was soon a hit in all our neighborhood games. Almost everyone wanted to switch gloves with me between innings of play. I still have this Bill Glynn autographed glove and until this past year knew nothing about the career of this player. After referencing a baseball encyclopedia I found out he was a first baseman that played in only 310 major league games. His major league highlight occurred on July 5, 1957 when he hit three, of his major league total of ten, home runs in one game for the Cleveland Indians. How he got his signature on a glove after such a short, rather uneventful career one may never know, but this type of story can provide hope for many a young athlete! Sometimes good things may happen, rather unexpectedly, if a player is willing to put in some practice.

As a seventh grader, I begged my father for a pair of $8.00 Chuck Taylor Converse sneakers. Back in 1965, these were the "Cadillac" of basketball sneakers. The only trouble was I was the oldest in a family with five children and had always worn P. F. Flyers, which were about half the price. I was able to purchase the "Cons," but only because I had performed some extra chores around the house. If I had not earned them, I would not have gotten these sneakers. There was no dickering with my father. In those days "no" meant "no." It might be a good idea to establish an annual sports budget for each child. Then if a child wishes to exceed the budget, he will have to pay the difference. This may force the child to go to a less expensive brand. By the time any three to four month sports season is over the equipment purchased probably will not be able to be used again because your child will have outgrown it. If you are talking about a baseball glove, lacrosse stick or something of this nature just wait until your kid comes home and tells you this piece of equipment was lost, stolen, or even left on a bus. At a time like this, you will be glad you went for the $25.99 glove as opposed to the $99.99 model "junior" so desperately needed or the $39.00 aluminum bat instead of the $99.00 model. A parent must be prepared to replace many pieces of equipment, which are lost or just "disappear." Speak openly to your child about these situations and do not be afraid to have him use some of his own money if a particular piece of equipment is a "must have." Additionally, if "junior" loses a piece of equipment or has it "stolen," he should help contribute towards the replacement cost. Many areas have used equipment stores where you can save a bundle on slightly used equipment. Also, check on the Internet, local classifieds or with friends and neighbors. It may take a little extra effort, but in the end it will have been well worth it. A parent's investment in a child's athletic wardrobe need not rival a 401K account.

I am pleased to say I was recently spared the expense of a new pair of cross-country shoes. This past fall my youngest found his oldest brother's three-year-old pair of cross-country spikes in our basement. He wore them for the entire season and I believe made his older brother proud. While home on a college break my oldest attended one of his younger brother's cross-country meets and remarked: "Well, I see you are wearing shoes that once belonged to 'The Legend'." (A legend in his own mind, no doubt!)

Another way for busy parents to save time and money is to car pool. Sometimes all it takes is a telephone call. All parents can use some extra time and it is certainly not necessary for a parent to sit and watch practice sessions. If you have observed that the coach runs a disciplined practice, is organized, and appears to be knowledgeable about the sport, you should recognize it after the first practice or two and feel comfortable leaving your child in his care. I am continually amazed at the number of parents who sit and watch entire practices or feel obligated to attend practice games. These are not performances and parents need not attend them all. Most parents give more than enough time to their children. If your child has a good coach, then take the time to accomplish some things for yourself or other members of the family.

A parent must constantly be aware of the officials at youth sporting events. Many organizations use junior high and high school athletes as officials and very often teenagers are given a huge responsibility without any training. It is imperative to keep the sporting event under control at all times and to know the rules! Officiating is not for the timid or shy. (The sponsoring organization as well as the teenage officials may have good intentions. However, if the officials are not loud and clear enough with their calls or do not like to blow the whistle, the game is likely to become unnecessarily rough. The result may be a group of coaches and parents becoming very upset.) Most parents I have spoken to agree that controlling the game and keeping it safe is the most important factor at the young age groups. If a game spirals out of control by getting exceedingly rough, someone will surely get hurt. All young officials must be trained to blow the whistle, when appropriate, and keep the game as safe as possible for all participants. The home team coaches, responsible for providing the officials, may often have to help on occasion to provide a fair interpretation of the rules. Younger, less experienced participants must also be "coached" by the officials with a proper explanation after every call. In addition, under no circumstances should children of the same age officiate in any contests where some of their peers may be participants. Several years ago at a local minor league baseball game, the opposing coach was responsible to provide the umpires. He did not take the time to find a parent in the stands and asked me, as the opposing coach, if he could use two little league players to call the game. My answer was an emphatic "no." I could tell that some of the parents from the opposing team were not too pleased with my answer, but I was confident I had given the correct one. Most of them may have been somewhat displeased because the coach would now be requesting their assistance to umpire the game. Oh, well! It would not be right to have two boys from a local little league umpiring a game against other boys who had been cut from the team earlier in the spring. Let us look at a situation that could have developed:

The home plate umpire calls a boy out on strikes. (The batter did not swing.) During school, the following day, the "umpire" brags he had called his classmate out on strikes the previous night. I am sure the contestant felt bad enough about not making the little league team and by striking out. Now a peer his age, who should not have been umpiring the game in the first place, has publicly humiliated him. This type of situation should always be avoided. "Kids must not officiate kids." Parents and high school students should be the officials at youth athletic contests.

As your child nears middle school age, very often "paid officials" will be used. A parent must be aware that this does not guarantee the game will be called in a flawless manner. All a parent can expect is that the officials appear enthusiastic and are trying their best. At times, an official may not be in a great frame of mind when arriving for the game due to a bad day at the office or the general pressures of life. However, just remember he will more than likely be unbiased so try to "stay off him" and let him do his job. I am reminded of an official who showed up at one of my recreation league basketball games. He stepped into the circle for the initial jump ball circle and remarked, "Okay, fellas, I have had a really miserable day today and really do not want to be here, so don't give me any crap." The WRONG thing to say! Even at this level of basketball, a comment such as this is inexcusable.

Now I would like to make parents aware of a few things which are out of your control, but of which you should certainly be aware. First, if the particular organization you are a member of provides some equipment be sure that it is relatively new and does not appear as if it were worn by Johnny Bench or Johnny Unitas. (Stars of the 1960s and 1970s with the Cincinnati Reds and Baltimore Colts, respectively.) The most important thing is that it is safe. For example, you do not want aluminum bats to have cracks in them, football or baseball helmets to have rotten or no padding, or soccer shin guards that are 4-5 years old. Additionally, the playing surface should be free of any foreign objects such as glass, nails or any type of metal or hard plastic material. Naturally, a well-worn soccer ball or basketball uniform is generally not a safety issue so there would be little cause for concern. Also, be sure to get your hands on the equipment and look it over well before your first game so you may address specific needs. Last year when I collected our baseball equipment from the community shed where everything is stored I found out a family of mice had taken up residence in the interior of a batting helmet stored within our equipment sack. One helmet's foam interior was chewed to shreds and the equipment sack looked as if it had taken a hit with birdshot from a twelve-gage shotgun. I will not describe how my car smelled during a brief ride home in eighty-degree weather, but can tell you I was doing all of my breathing through my mouth!

If the coach does not have an able-bodied assistant, it would be wise to check and see if he is planning to recruit one. This might not be as important for a seven or eight person basketball team, as it is for a much larger soccer or football team, but for organizational purposes, it is essential. The assistant does not have to be as well versed in the particulars of the sport, but he must be able to instruct the children on proper "bench behavior" and be able to discipline them, as required. This adult MUST be able to say the word "NO" to children and instruct them about proper bench behavior.

Every coach should have a first aid kit at all practices and games. At a minimum, the kit should include bandages, an antiseptic, gauze, some ice packs, plastic gloves, and some athletic tape. If real ice is made available, it is much more effective for sprains, bumps, and bruises than the artificial ice packs. Perhaps the coach or assistant could take a small cooler packed with some ice, plastic bags, and some wet washcloths to every game and practice. Many schools and communities are now also requiring defibrillators in case a child goes into cardiac arrest. However, at the present time, these units are cost prohibitive for many schools and organizations. There should also be a person on site who has been properly trained on the use of a defibrillator.

Most youth athletic organizations have a blanket insurance policy covering all the youth involved. Additionally, the coaches and organization administrators should be covered in case of any liability lawsuits. For your peace of mind, you may want to ask for the particulars regarding what insurance company is involved and what types of limits are in effect. The easiest way to do this is to ask to have a copy of a certificate of insurance or at the least to be able to see one and perhaps write down the pertinent information. You must be sure that the young athlete, as well as yourself (if you coach), is adequately protected by insurance.

Parents must also be aware that with the decline of the three-sport athlete in today's society a child may tire of a sport if he is doing it year round. Some children do "burnout," losing the desire to compete. This can occur at a variety of age levels. It may occur when a child is entering the seventh or eighth grade or after high school. A friend on my high school basketball team who I felt was a much better player than I had no desire to even tryout for his college team, yet my desire to play as a seventeen-year-old was unquenchable.

As a parent, recognize that most sports activities your child is involved with are probably adult organized and adult supervised. There is not the myriad of "sandlot" baseball games, backyard wiffle-ball games, or pickup basketball games in the park we used to witness decades ago. These types of "disorganized" (by today's standards) games were often very constructive, as children had to work things out by themselves if disputes or arguments arose. Yes, at times fisticuffs may have resulted, but this was also part of an individual's growth. I can remember disputes arising over the picking of teams, the home run boundary, the number of innings or the time the game would end, etc., etc. My best friend once heaved my new glove into our pool all because of a call I made during a wiffle ball game! We were both sixteen years old when this happened! Everything was usually worked out without incident and, as youngsters, we became more competent in handling disagreements because there were no adults to interfere. Recently, when I was speaking to a friend about trying to encourage boys to play sports when school is out she said, "Maybe parents need to take the time to 'organize' pickup ball." I smiled at this because the statement was an oxymoron. "Pickup," in this case is defined as, "using available personnel without formal organization." As adults, many cannot get away from ORGANIZING things for our children. How will the youngsters ever learn to be creative and learn to solve things for themselves if the adults keep doing it for them? Neighborhood games and pickup ball still offer advantages! These types of games generally sport a limited number of players thus allowing for more touches of the ball, more at bats, more shots, etc. etc. All of these are individual skills and require this type of repetition to become a better athlete. Thirty-five years later I can still hear my mom shouting, "Will you boys get outta here and go play some ball or something?" Most of the time we were happy to oblige.

Also keep in mind, that for the very young (under 10), there is never a need for coaches (or parents for that matter) to spend a great deal of time on a critical post game rehash. A post game cheer or an occasional celebration, whether win, lose, or draw, is also a good idea. The most important thing is that a group of children were PLAYING A GAME and having fun!

AFTERTHOUGHTS

It has taken almost fifty years to garner all my thoughts and experiences to make this a worthwhile publication. A few things I have heard about and witnessed just over the past couple of years have only strengthened my conviction to bring it to fruition. Numerous Internet sites exist which are devoted to youth sports, but none touch on all the issues I have addressed in this generic publication. I have referred to many real life situations I have encountered over the years so you may learn from them. You can refer to this book for advice as your child matures. I felt the need to inform parents of young athletes about what they are getting into, as well as some uncomfortable situations that may develop. Additionally, the behavior of many adults, both coaches and spectators, has been despicable and needs vast improvement. Perhaps I have shed some light on situations you have already or will soon experience. I hope that my commentary and suggestions will allow you to better deal with various situations as they arise.

All amateur athletic programs, at any level, should strive to provide an opportunity for our youth to learn and grow. As a child nears middle school age the word "competition" will rear its somewhat ugly head, but this is a part of life and can often be something for a child to learn from and mature. As we all know in order to grow and develop, pain is often necessary. However, it can be a difficult balancing act.

There is no getting around the subject of competition, as it is an integral part of sports. Most of the time no one wants to take part in a game when a score is irrelevant. Just keep in mind that winning is only part of the game, and over the course of time, may not be the most important part of what a youngster may learn from athletics. An adolescent's games are not performances, or World Series games or Superbowls. They are only games! These are only events where he is hopefully having fun and burning off some energy.

However, such aforementioned terms of teamwork, discipline, organization, sportsmanship and persistence will be useful skills a child can take forward in life. The benefits of athletics extend far beyond words like "competition" and "winning." A placard I spotted a short time ago in a middle school physical education teacher's office read:

"Education + Athletics = Success"

This short phrase says a lot! A child must be a student first. Athletics provide great extracurricular activities that have the potential to teach valuable lessons to last a lifetime. They might be lessons that will never be taught in a classroom. In fact, the participation on a sports team is seen by many to be an extension of the classroom.

"Curiosity and play should be used to promote learning."
Jean Jaques Rosseau

The following story about the late North Carolina State basketball coach Jimmy Valvano supports the overall theme of this publication.

Early in 1993, Valvano, suffering from terminal spinal cancer, shared a few of his prior coaching experiences with a reporter. He recounted a story about a college basketball team he had coached twenty –three years earlier at the age of twenty-four.

One day a player approached him after practice and asked, "Why is winning that important to you?"

"Because the final score defines you. You lose, ergo; you're a loser. You win, ergo, you're a winner," Valvano replied.

"No," the player responded, "participation is the key. Trying your best, regardless of whether you win or lose, that is what defines you."

Valvano's memory of a day long past ended here.

Twenty-four years later, his life dangling by a thread, this young player's words finally affected him. After jumping out of bed on numerous occasions with a sweat-filled tee shirt, shivering from the effects of the dreaded chemotherapy treatments, and experiencing horrifying dreams of seeing himself die over and over again he realized something.

"That player was right," he told the reporter. "It's the effort, not the result. It's trying your best. God, what a great human being I could have been if I had been aware of this back then."

Valvano died regretting he did not heed a young player's advice early in his career.

This short story should help to put a few things in perspective for parents, coaches, and spectators.

Look at the BIG picture. Your child has the opportunity to play a sport. He is physically and mentally able to do so. He may try his very best and give it all he has, but never be an all-star. He may *leave it all on the field* and his team still may never be number one. In spite of all this, he may end up the better for it by knowing how to handle defeat better somewhere down the road. If he has the DESIRE, there will always be another sport, another event, and another team. For now, be thankful for the opportunity that he had to be able to PLAY the games. It should be PLAY, for it should not be work, a bother, or a career. If it is not fun, something is awry and the scenario should be reevaluated. Parents should strive to make the sports experience a positive and rewarding one for every young participant. In a few circumstances, it may mean respecting a young child's wishes to drop off a team and try something else. A parent must recognize that there is no guarantee a child will excel at or even enjoy a particular sport. However, you must be aware that neither of these is necessary to be successful as a human being. At the youngest of ages, sports MUST be viewed as a diversion, an extracurricular activity, and nothing more.

I would like to close by remembering the words often used by a fellow parishioner who lost both of his legs as a very young man while serving this country at sea:

"Be thankful for what you have."
Harold Lee

If someone with this type of misfortune can look at life in this manner, should we not be able to do the same? A parent must remember that youth sports constitute a fleeting moment in time and are only a portion of a child's total development.

Good luck in your adventure through the world of youth sports!

GLOSSARY OF TERMS

A. D. – short for athletic director

Beehive soccer – all the young athletes swarm around the ball like bees around a hive

Between the lines – participating in an athletic event (i.e. between the sidelines during a football game or between the foul lines during a baseball game)

Bomb squad time – the last two or three minutes of a basketball game when players who rarely get in are able to show their stuff. Many are often only interested in squeezing off ill-advised shots from long range often referred to as "bombs."

BP – slang for batting practice

Call off the dogs – the point spread is so great, time is running out, and the ballgame is over. (The opponent is "dead.") Another phrase, often used, is "start the bus" once a victory is assured.

Cutthroat – marked by unprincipled practice, a ruthless competitor to gain an advantage or victory.

Field of play – an area marked for sports play

Grain of salt – a skeptical attitude

Gym rat – a person who always seems to be in a gymnasium

whenever it is open

Hot – a synonym for angry which an athlete will often use

Jock – slang term for an athlete. (This was at one time a vital piece of a boy's athletic wear a few decades ago, but I think sales have slipped.)

Keeper – another name for a goalkeeper or goalie on a soccer team

Late bloomer – physically, and perhaps mentally, behind in athletic skill development compared to peers

Leave it all on the field – giving all one has to give during an athletic event, sparing nothing

Magnetic basketball – very similar to beehive soccer, but in a different sport. The magnet is the basketball and the young athletes are like paperclips.

Monday morning quarterback – one who second-guesses or critically rehashes a game already completed.

Pigeonhole – to assign to a category (or in regards to athletics – assign to a position)

Pine – this is what a team bench is often referred to because most of them used to be made of pinewood.
P. T. – playing time (Recently some sports announcers have duplicated the use of this abbreviation as "prime time," or the tail end of a contest where all plays become magnified.)

Pulls the ball – a baseball or softball term for hitting the ball to the strong side, which is towards right field for left-handed batters and towards left field for right-handed batters. If one does not pull the ball, it is often said the hitter swung late or "took the ball the opposite way."

Rubber meets the road – this is when the reality of the situation kicks in. The reason the game is played is to declare a victor.

Scrimmage – practice play between two separate squads, simulates a game

Shirts & skins – one boy's team would shed their shirts to distinguish themselves from the opposition, an impromptu uniform

Showboating – to behave in a vainglorious (boastful) manner, unwarranted and exaggerated behavior

Syracuse sprints – nowadays often referred to as "suicides." A sprint beginning on the baseline under one basket, a player would run to the foul line back to the baseline, to half court and back to the baseline, to the opposite foul line and back to the baseline, and finally to the opposite baseline and back to the original baseline. (On a long court, do you see why these could also be called "suicides"?)

The "W" – to WIN an athletic contest
Thick skinned – impervious to criticism

Throw in the towel – to acknowledge defeat, abandon the

struggle

Tomfoolery – Playful or foolish behavior, may also describe a situation when some members of a team are involved in a lot of small talk, pranks, and fooling around. Not paying attention to the coach, practice, or game.

Walk-ons – non-scholarship players who have made the team

Washed up – beyond one's peak performance years, at the end of a career

Wally Pipp – an eleven-year veteran of the New York Yankees and starting first baseman who, due to a headache, asked for a day off in 1925. His replacement, young Lou Gehrig, remained in the lineup for 2,130 straight games. A year or so later Pipp was traded to the Cincinnati Reds and labored in obscurity.

Printed in the United Kingdom
by Lightning Source UK Ltd.
111782UKS00001B/87